TURN IT OFF

TURN

How to Unplug from the

Anytime-Anywhere Office

Without Disconnecting

from Your Career

IT OFF

GIL E. GORDON

THREE RIVERS PRESS
NEW YORK

Thanks to Ken Dulaney of Gartner Group Inc. for permission to use excerpts from his presentation material in Chapter 8. The excerpts are reprinted by permission, and are copyright © 2000 Gartner Group Inc. All rights reserved.

Published by Three Rivers Press, New York, New York.
Member of the Crown Publishing Group.

Random House, Inc. New York, Toronto, London, Sydney, Auckland
www.randomhouse.com

THREE RIVERS PRESS is a registered trademark and the Three Rivers Press colophon is a trademark of Random House, Inc.

Printed in the United States of America

Design by LEONARD HENDERSON

Library of Congress Cataloging-in-Publication Data
Gordon, Gil E.
    Turn it off: how to unplug from the anytime-anywhere office without disconnecting from your career / Gil Gordon—1st ed.
        1. Time management.   2. Telecommunication—Management.   I. Title.
HD69.T54 G67   2001
650.1—dc21
                                                            00-064775

ISBN 0-609-806971

10   9   8   7   6   5   4   3   2

First Edition

CONTENTS

ACKNOWLEDGMENTS

Most authors end their acknowledgments with a "last but not least" recognition of their spouse and family. That would be completely inappropriate in this book for reasons that I hope will become obvious to you as you read it. My wife, Ellen, and our children, Lisa and Adam, are largely responsible for this book; without them I would have many fewer reasons to work less and start enjoying life more.

Beyond my family, I owe my sincere thanks and gratitude to:

John Brennan, Bob Long, Janice Miholics, Susan Sweet, and—especially—Paul Rupert, who all reviewed a near-final draft of this book and let me know where I was off track and what I needed to do to make the book more credible and useful. I am most thankful for the time they took and for their candor.

Nick Brealey, who also reviewed a draft and, with a true publisher's eye, pinpointed exactly what was wrong and, better yet, exactly how to fix it.

Liv Blumer of the Karpfinger Agency, who was not only the best kind of advocate I could hope for, but who also gave me ongoing direction, encouragement, and critique in a way that made me look forward to each contact with her.

Becky Cabaza of Three Rivers Press, who has guided this book through the final editing and production processes and made me feel that she was at least as interested in seeing this book come off the press as I was, and who has a perfect talent for spotting what needed improvement.

Paul Edwards, whose long-term friendship and e-mail correspondence has been a source of excellent advice and refreshing humor, and who has been my long-distance sounding board and confidant for close to two decades.

Paul Saffo, a man for whom the terms "futurist" and "visionary" don't begin to describe his unique talents, for all the things he has said and done over the years to inspire me to write this book.

Dave Fleming, a colleague who disproves the theory that people who live far apart from each other can't develop close and trusting professional relationships and personal friendships.

Sue Shellenbarger, whose remarkably insightful and balanced coverage of work and family issues for the *Wall Street Journal* gives me a weekly energy boost and intellectual challenge.

Michael Fatali, who introduced me to the joys of landscape photography and so willingly shared his time and skills in a way that helped me discover the beauty of nature and the nature of beauty.

Richard Bird, Bill Bronkan, Al Kocourek, Tom Massey, and Dan McGuire, with whom I have had the pleasure of sharing various hiking and landscape photography trips in the Southwest. They have helped me enjoy the land, put up with my travel planning and map fetish, and have become very special kinds of friends with whom I enjoy time when I "turn it off" and get away from work, my office, and everything electronic.

To all these people, and to countless clients and colleagues whose various ideas and comments over the years have stimulated and shaped my thinking, I am grateful beyond words.

TURN IT OFF

CHAPTER 1

How *Did* We Become So Attached to Our Offices?

None of us wakes up one day and decides, "I think I'll give up my free time on weekends, answer my pages during dinner with my spouse, and carry my laptop on vacation." Those intrusions of work into our personal time result from a process of slow erosion, not sudden upheaval. As employees, we ourselves have unwittingly contributed to that process and ended up stretching our workdays and workweeks.

One of the characteristics of office work up to the 1980s (and thus before the deluge of technology) was the containment of most office work within the office. Certainly, the briefcases came home, the traveling businessperson worked on a plane or in a hotel room, and the sales rep caught up on paperwork in the car. But when far less office work was as easily portable as it is today, the types of work that could be packed into that briefcase were much more limited.

Employees who still had items on their to-do lists at 5 P.M. were more likely to stay late in the office than to simply pack up the briefcase and plan to finish everything after dinner. Briefcases weren't big enough to contain a file drawer's worth of information, and there was no easy way to look at a set of engineering drawings or a year's worth of monthly budget printouts on the kitchen table. At-home evening and weekend work was mostly limited to reading, drafting memos and reports on yellow pads, and grinding out budgets using a pocket calculator—absolutely archaic activities by today's standards.

If we fast-forward to the late 1990s, we can see that the limitations on the kinds of work that could be done from afar disappeared almost entirely. Looking for the sales reports from the last two quarters? Just log on to the corporate network and download the files. Need to get out a rush memo to the entire sales force? Draft it on your laptop and upload it to the mail server, and it's in the sales reps' mailboxes in seconds. While every aspect of every job was not portable, enough were to enable most office workers to leave at a more desirable hour, get home in time for dinner, and still be able to finish the day's work at home after having had at least a little time with the spouse or family over the dinner table.

So far so good—until the point when those of us taking work home slipped into some bad habits. The idea that came to us for the new marketing campaign could now be sketched out on the laptop at 10 P.M.—instead of being hastily scribbled down on a note to be taken into the office and worked on the next day. The budget planning that was going on with the overseas offices could now be compressed from weeks to days because global fax and e-mail meant that the morning message sent from Tokyo could be read in the evening—at home—by the financial analyst from the New York office, and so on.

You might ask, "What's wrong with that? Isn't business life today all about doing things faster and faster? Isn't it *good* to be able to save time by taking advantage of these tools?" The answer is, of course, yes—but I believe it's a qualified yes. No doubt there are times when a faster response is not only better but absolutely essential. The problem arises when the people involved don't differentiate between the value of and need for having it faster on one hand and the desire to have it faster just because someone *can* send that e-mail from home at 11 P.M.

There are many benefits to being able to work extended hours at home instead of staying until all hours in the office and making do with a vending machine sandwich for dinner while your spouse or family stares at your empty chair at the table. It's great to be able to do increasingly sophisticated, complex office work at home; it's not so great when we aren't able to close the door (literally or figuratively) on the home office and wind up working well into time we'd rather reserve for ourselves.

Why I Wrote This Book

I am quick to note that I've been as guilty as anyone about failing to maintain the separation between work and the rest of my life. To give one example, I distinctly remember my "telephone sprints" during the first two years or so after I started my home-based consulting business in 1982, after spending almost ten years in the corporate world. My office is downstairs and the main living area is upstairs in our house; when I'd go up for lunch I'd be reluctant to turn on the telephone answering machine for fear that I'd miss the big call that would bring me fame and fortune—or at least a little bit of consulting work. At that time in my fledgling business, *every* call was a "big call" because things were, to put it mildly, slow.

I'd be up in the kitchen having lunch and would hear the office phone ring, and would drop my sandwich in mid-bite and fly down the stairs, risking life and limb to get to the phone before that prospective client gave up and hung up. It's a wonder I didn't break any bones. It took me two full years before I realized I could give myself the luxury of an uninterrupted lunch break in my own home simply by turning on the answering machine.

As the technology I used became more complex and more integral over the years, it became evident to me how my technology-enabled work was squeezing free time out of my life, and squeezing me out of my family's life. I became intrigued with how common these problems were for others as well and started paying serious attention to work-life boundary issues in the early 1990s. They were becoming especially evident in my work with my *Fortune* 100–class corporate clients implementing telecommuting or telework programs. Those experiences, plus my observations of "road warriors" doing work at unusual times in unusual places, prompted me to bring this book to life.

In particular, I noticed the following signs and symptoms as I worked with my corporate clients:

- People seemed to be increasingly stretched, stressed, and almost breathless as they made their way from week to week. I would walk into a client's office for a Monday-morning meeting and almost everyone looked and acted as if it were 5 P.M. on Friday afternoon.

- I began to get e-mail and voice mail messages that had been sent late into the evening or on the weekend—and in some cases on holiday weekends or during times when I knew a particular client was on vacation.

- The excitement with which people used to describe the tools they used (laptops, cell phones, e-mail, and so on) was replaced with a sense of resignation or even resentment. It was no longer, "This is really great! She was able to e-mail me the budget so I could work on it at home." Instead, it was, "Can you believe it? She e-mailed me the budget at 9 P.M. one night and expected me to have the updates done and back in her e-mail box before her 7 A.M. meeting the next morning!"

In addition to these observations, the most compelling reason for writing the book was seeing the reactions when I told colleagues and clients about it. I'd mention that I was starting a new book, and the title words *Turn It Off* were barely out of my mouth before I'd see the person's eyes open wide, followed by a knowing nod of appreciation of the problem that the title implied. Then I'd hear them say something like "Boy, do I need that book—now!" or "I can think of a couple of people who should read it," which confirmed their interest. The fact that this issue was so much in their awareness, and that so many people seemed trapped by the long hours and almost endless work, convinced me that the time was right for this book.

The three background factors I'll review shortly help explain why I'm seeing what I did, and why, perhaps, you feel like you do. You'll see throughout the book that my goal is to help you assess your own situation and decide *if and to what extent* you want to change—and then I'll help you put a plan together and show you how to implement it.

I want to make it clear that while my own experiences have caused me to choose a lifestyle that gives me a more distinct—but still imperfect—separation between work and the rest of my life, I realize that you might see things differently. That's my way of saying that you'll get insights and information from this book—but no moralizing, prescribing, or finger-wagging from me. On the other hand, I'm completely confident that you'll find all the tips and methods you need if you *do* want to make some changes. I've seen these concepts work for my corporate clients and they'll work for you as well.

I'm not entirely sure what thought process leads someone who is probably already feeling overworked to take *more* work to places we normally think of as being work-free, but it is happening more often. Perhaps it's the notion that work squeezed in when there's a break in the action at these places is work that doesn't have to be done later, elsewhere. Perhaps it's a conscious or subconscious desire to be seen as so vitally important that work follow everywhere. And perhaps it's our new-age way of supercharging our lives by stretching our capacity for work, play, entertainment, and family time all at once. The technology lets us add hours to the day, and diversions and distractions to our lives.

No matter how diverse or seemingly justified the reasons, we become the ultimate multitaskers. Instead of concentrating on and savoring the pleasures of the moment in depth, we end up leading high-bandwidth, low-fidelity lives. This may well be the lifestyle of choice for some, but I suspect that for many it is a pattern they have slipped into and not one they consciously and deliberately chose.

Tracing the Trends

In offices and at work, as in all parts of our lives, we're immersed in a set of changes that were barely foreseen just a few years ago—and they go far beyond technology. Many of us often feel overwhelmed by the sheer volume of technology that surrounds us, the pace at which we're expected to absorb it, and the number of things that fill up our to-do lists for our lives, not just our jobs.

(This is one reason, incidentally, why the simplification movement has become so popular in the last few years. This is a response to the way many of us feel our lives have spun out of control, and that we are now a slave to and not a master of our lifestyles. While this is a noteworthy social phenomenon, and is somewhat related to the focus of this book, we'll be concentrating on the workplace and the ways in which our work and our lives are intertwined.)

Setting simplicity aside, let's look at the three major factors behind the "de-officing" of office work and the disappearance of time boundaries for office workers:

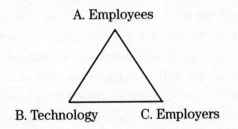

A. Employees

B. Technology   C. Employers

As we review each factor, you'll better understand how we got into this situation and why simplistic solutions just won't suffice.

A. *Employees: Do It All, Want It All, Have It All*

The first corner of the triangle that forms the basis of our tendency to work almost without limits is the shift in employee and labor force values, interests, and goals. Not only has the technology changed so we *can* work almost anywhere and anytime, and employers have changed so we're *expected to* work almost anywhere and anytime (as you'll see later in this chapter)—we as individuals are changing so that many of us actually *want to be able to* work almost anywhere and anytime.

One source of this is what I call "defensive overwork." There are many reasons why people consistently work long hours and in some cases become true workaholics. One reason that is relatively new is the sometimes irrational but perfectly understandable reaction to the relatively recent history of downsizing.

When the word goes out that an employer is going to reengineer, restructure, or re-whatever, almost all employees get a twinge of fear as they wonder if they'll get caught in the downsizing downdraft. Performance records, plaudits, and praise from managers and co-workers aside, the reality is that downsizing can strike anyone. When the news release says that "4,000 employees will lose their jobs," it doesn't say, "the 4,000 employees *with the worst ratings* will lose their jobs." The extent to which the stream of downsizing that started in the late 1980s has made employees feel that the guillotine is always swinging uncomfortably close to their own necks is a sad commentary on organizational life, but that's the reality.

What do many employees do when faced with the possibility of being out of a job and out on the street—in some cases for the first time in ten years or more? No matter what assurances their bosses may offer, most employees will redouble their efforts and do whatever they can to show that *their* performance is too valuable to lose. In some cases, this means that an average employee can truly raise his or her performance to a superior level, but in many cases it can be nothing more than a lot of extra (and, ideally, highly visible) work and activity. Better to look like you're sweating and slaving away for the good of the organization than to risk being labeled as "not a team player" or "doesn't seem to want to do whatever is needed to get the job done."

Where does a lot of this defensive overwork get done? At home, of course—in the evening, on the weekend, and even if you're sick in bed with the flu. It may also be why some people who in the mid-1980s would never have dreamed of interrupting their vacation to contact the office now carry a pager and check their voice mail and e-mail from the hotel room at the beach or wherever they went for a vacation *from* the office.

Compounding this is what we do in response to impositions on our own time by others. This kind of "accidental reinforcement" is a perfect example of the saying about being our own worst enemies.

We all know about the basics of behavior reinforcement: if we're rewarded (or at least not punished) for doing something, we'll tend to do it again; if we're punished (or at least not rewarded) for doing something, we'll tend not to do it again. That works for mice in a laboratory maze, small

The Sunday-Afternoon Intrusion

What happened the last time your boss or an important client called you at home on a Sunday afternoon or any other time over the weekend?

A. It never happens.
B. I always use my answering machine or voice mail to screen my calls on the weekend; this is how I avoid those unwanted calls.
C. I answered the call and talked to the boss for 20 minutes—and was gritting my teeth all the while.
D. I turned up the volume on the TV and made it sound like I had friends over watching the game; my boss felt guilty and cut the call short.
E. I answered the call, and when I heard what the boss wanted I flew off the handle and made it *very* clear how I felt about having my weekend disrupted.
F. I answered the call, heard what the boss wanted, gave a short but complete answer, and then told the boss that I'd prefer in the future that we wait to discuss matters like this until Monday unless it was truly an emergency, and that I'd be glad to sit down with him or her to talk about this first thing Monday morning.

If you answered A you're either lucky that you don't face this problem, or you have faced it in the past and worked out an alternative with your boss or clients. If you answered B or C or D you're avoiding the issue—and it isn't going to go away. If you answered E you may have avoided the interruption but you probably didn't do much good for your career.

If you answered F give yourself a pat on the back; you gave the boss the answer that was needed, and in doing so made it clear that you didn't appreciate the intrusion and would like to resolve this issue when you both return to the office. This isn't always an easy conversation to have, but it's the only way you can be assured of letting the boss know how you value your time away from work.

children who decide to exercise their artistic talents with crayons on the living-room wall—and also for managers who call their employees at home on Sunday morning.

Every time the boss, or a customer or co-worker, calls you on a Sunday morning, pages you to remind you to check your e-mail at 11 P.M., or e-mails you an assignment while you're on vacation, you have a choice to make. If you respond (perhaps understandably) to these requests, you are inadvertently reinforcing that person's attempt to turn some of your personal time back into work time. Chances are the person realizes he or she is about to invade what *should* be your free time, and may even have a moment's hesitation before sending that page or calling you. If you respond without letting it be known that you dislike the intrusion, that intruder is very likely to think, "Well, he didn't *say* anything about my calling on Sunday morning," or "She *did* check her e-mail from the ski lodge and got me the numbers I wanted." The result? This person will hesitate much less, and perhaps not at all, the next time he or she considers calling or paging you on the weekend or late at night.

In Chapter 6, we'll cover some specific ways to discuss your concerns about incidents like these with your boss or customers or whomever—but for now, understand the role that this kind of accidental reinforcement plays in perpetuating these incidents. I'm not suggesting for a moment that you arbitrarily ignore the page, slam down the phone, or delete the e-mail—those are prescriptions for career suicide. And assuming that these requests and interruptions are at least somewhat justified, if not highly urgent, you'd be foolish to think you can maintain the boundary around your free time without causing problems for the organization.

For now, though, it's more important to understand how much we do to bring some of these endless work problems on ourselves, albeit quite unintentionally. Though some of you might not mind getting those evening or weekend calls or messages, others most definitely do find them to be out of place. Later, we'll look further into ways to make these "reach out and find you" technologies work well without having them overtake your life.

THE EMPLOYEE BOTTOM LINE

It may be that *we* put ourselves into this boundaryless lifestyle with little or no separation between our work and personal lives. Even if that's true, it's not the only factor that affects what we as individuals do in concert with the changes in technology and employers. So don't feel guilty if you've been spotted sorting through your e-mail inbox between acts of a school play.

I do think we should realize that while it's tempting to localize the source of the problem with the "they"—*they* keep giving me more work, *they* put power outlets near airplane seats so our work hours can exceed our battery levels, and so on—it's likely that *we* own part of the problem, too. The good news is that if we own it, we can change it, or at least the part that's under our direct control—and that's exactly how this book will help you.

B. Technology: Smaller, Faster, Cheaper, Better

We have moved from the veritable Stone Age of technology to the current situation in relatively few years. To see how quickly we've progressed, let's view technology through the experiences of three different groups of students—certainly some of the most astute consumers of hardware, software, phone lines, and all the rest. Consider a typical technology profile for these three groups (separated by only five years) at the start of the new century:

1. *Students born in 1982* and in their first year in a college in 2000 never knew a time when they didn't have a VCR, desktop computer, cordless phone (and perhaps a cell phone) and answering machine (or voice mail) at their fingertips at home, and a computer in or near their classroom at school from their earliest school years on up.

They may remember listening to music on cassette tapes, instead relying almost exclusively on compact discs and, more recently, MP3 downloads from the Internet. Most important, they relied on the Internet for help with homework and for entertainment—not to mention the time spent in chat rooms and IM'ing (or "instant messaging" for the rest of us) with their friends.

2. *Students born in 1977* and in their first year of post-college employment in 2000 grew up with most of those same tools nearby, did most of their library research without ever setting foot in the college library, submitted their assignments over the school's network, and in many cases took their classroom notes by tapping on a laptop instead of writing in a notebook.

They may have arrived at the college with their collection of cassette tapes but left with only CDs and downloaded files. The Internet crept into their college days slowly but surely, and they took to it like ducks to water.

3. *Former students born in 1972* and in their fifth year of post-college employment in 2000 may not have been as immersed in all that technology while growing up and in their college years, but have certainly plunged into it at the office. While growing up they may have actually listened to vinyl record albums—a format for which they probably couldn't find a player nearby today even if they wanted to.

During their five years of employment, they have seen up to three successive PCs on their desktops, each more powerful than the last, and perhaps are now using a laptop with a docking station at home and in the office. Many of them routinely carry alphanumeric pagers, personal digital assistants (PDAs), and cell phones. They probably spend as much time on their corporate intranets as on the Internet, and may have multiple e-mail accounts because they've figured out that's how to subvert their employer's right to electronically eavesdrop on their e-mail.

We could continue with this technology analysis in five-year increments but you get the idea: as immersed as today's children and teenagers are in computing and telecommunications technology, their older siblings and, perhaps, even their parents are quickly becoming almost equally wired.

As dramatically as the equipment sales that foster mobile work have grown, wireless telecommunications access and broadband, or high-speed, access seem to be growing even faster. This is relevant to the "anytime-anywhere" workplace for two reasons:

1. An Insatiable Appetite for Bandwidth. What used to be slow is now intolerable, what used to be fast is now slow, and what now is generally recognized as ultra-fast (e.g., DSL lines or cable modems into the home) is desirable but still not widely available. The deployment of these faster-access methods will improve quickly, but will soon be supplanted by something even faster.

This bandwidth chase is especially relevant when we're considering locations beyond the four walls of the traditional office. Having high-speed access to the Internet or intranet via the corporate network while in the office is assumed to be a given these days; having anything near that speed when working at home or in a hotel room is still the exception as we begin the new century.

But the speed gap between the office and the remote sites is closing; as it does, more people are able—and might be tempted—to do more kinds of work remotely. The big spreadsheet or graphics file that you might have waited to download until your next trip into the office can now be fetched almost as quickly from the computer in your spare bedroom—*if* you have a cable modem, DSL line, or other form of broadband access.

2. Wired Versus Wireless: Portability + Speed = Freedom. Except for the times when they're trapped in one of the infamous cellular "dead zones," cell phone users are a pretty satisfied lot. They can call, or be called, from just about anywhere using a phone that can't get any smaller unless we shrink our fingertips—not a bad deal. You'd be hard pressed to find another innovation that has caught on so quickly, is used so often, and has extended the reach of the office so well.

But if a cell phone user puts a cellular modem in a laptop and dials up the corporate LAN or Internet service provider, things come to a grinding halt. A typical maximum speed for a cellular modem today is approximately the same speed as with most standard dial-up connections, though the actual speed you get will vary widely based on nearby cellular coverage and competing users.

Given the growth in DSL lines and cable modems, many remote workers at home or even in airport business centers and hotel rooms routinely get speeds that are many times faster.

Yes, you *can* sit with your cellular modem–equipped laptop in an airport and check your e-mail or upload a file—but it won't be much fun to do it at 28.8k bps. People enjoy bandwidth like wine; once they've tasted the good stuff, it's terribly hard to go back to the ordinary.

This low-speed barrier will soon be breached, as almost all technology barriers are. Even without that advance, though, the mobile worker can still get by with voice-only cell access—not to mention the next-generation cell service and phones that will deliver rudimentary Web access to a palm-sized phone.

The Special Role of the Cell Phone: Insights from the Inventor

The cell phone has without doubt become a pivotal tool in the mobile worker's toolkit. Though we're enamored with today's tiny, full-featured cell phones, it's worth noting that our experiences with cell phones today have a very long (by technology standards, at least) history that goes back to 1973. That's when Martin Cooper, then with Motorola, made the first call on a bulky handheld cell phone while standing on a street in Manhattan.

I asked Cooper to think back to those early days and comment on the changes he has seen. "This may surprise some people, but I always envisioned cellular phones as being portable, not something that we'd use in an office or in a car," he told me. "That's how they started being used, and I wasn't surprised at all that within five years, most of the units sold were portables. Today you can't even buy a car phone in the sense that we used to see them."

Cooper has some definite opinions about our use, or misuse, of technologies like the cell phone—and also made a point that underscores the theme of this book: "We're letting the technology control us instead of us controlling the technology. There's no reason why we should be obligated to answer a ringing cell phone just because we can—we have to remember to turn it off. But, as we've seen in the past, social change takes a lot longer to occur than technological change."

The Technology Bottom Line

Other than someone whose enjoyment of a movie has been interrupted by the electronic chirping of a cell phone, or whose long-awaited nap on a commuter train was punctuated by keys clicking on a seatmate's laptop, it would be hard to find anyone who isn't a fan of mobile-office technology—myself included.

As we have untethered ourselves from the wires and cables of the office and from the clunky desktop computers, we have virtually erased the boundary that had existed between work and personal life. Sales reps, engineers, consultants, and a host of others whose work took them into the field were always able to do some office work away from the office, but it took the technology advances of the 1980s and 1990s to let many others make a similar shift.

This trend has become so pronounced that employers all over the world are actively rethinking their need for having (and paying for) office space in direct proportion to employee headcount. The days of a one-to-one ratio of cubicles or offices to employees are fast disappearing as employers adopt cost-reducing facilities planning concepts such as hoteling or free-address offices (in which mobile employees use space on a drop-in basis as needed, and/or move around the office and have *a* space to work but not their *own* space). "Give the employees a laptop, a cell phone, and a pager, and let them work from just about anywhere" is the rallying cry. Unfortunately, the unspoken addition to that phrase is ". . . and just about anytime."

C. Employers: Downsizing, Squeezing, Globalizing, Speeding Up

The 1990s was a time when employers in the United States and many other countries discovered the thrills and spills of downsizing and rightsizing. United States employers reduced their staffing levels by tens of thousands of people in the 1990s. These cuts do not, of course, take into account the effects of any new job growth—just the numbers of people who were told their jobs had disappeared.

I have no doubt that much of this downsizing was needed—and long overdue, in some cases. My concern throughout that period and to this day is that many employers made two fundamental mistakes with their downsizing programs:

- Goodbye, Talent—Hello, Mediocrity. Employers lost many of the people they should have kept and kept many of the people they should have lost. As a result, some of the best and brightest employees literally took the money and ran when offered voluntary separation packages. Those who were more risk-averse and perhaps felt their skills weren't quite as marketable stayed on the payroll. Thus, the very people sorely needed by most employers to get them through the tough times of the last decade walked out the door, leaving the loyal but less stellar performers behind to pick up the slack.
- The People Left—The Work Remained. There were precious few employers who really understood that downsizing was not only about lopping off headcount but should

also have been an opportunity to evaluate and perhaps downsize the workload itself. This was the true meaning of the term "reengineering," which unfortunately became a euphemism for wholesale layoffs that occurred without the redesign of methods and procedures that should have accompanied them.

Granted, many companies came into the 1990s having become somewhat bloated, the result of previous decades when competitive pressures and scrutiny from Wall Street analysts weren't quite as relentless. However, if the people went away but the same tasks, to be done the same way, remained, the result was a mad dash to cram more work into fewer people. If six people are doing the work that ten used to do, and at the same time are expected to meet or exceed previous budget and productivity targets, something has to give. Staffing levels might have been a bit generous in years past, but that doesn't mean *everyone* was sitting around filing their nails and working a 35-hour workweek.

To this pressure-cooker environment in which everyone was supposed to "do more with less," we can add the globalization trend that swept through corporate boardrooms. It was as if CEOs awoke from a deep sleep and realized their competitors and customers were not only down the street or across the country, but just as likely to be across an ocean or two. To the extent that those competitors had a lower cost structure—which many did because their labor costs were so much lower—U.S. and European firms had yet another reason to keep budgets and headcounts lower.

The final ingredient in this stew of workplace turmoil was

fierce competition, which resulted in the pressure to do everything faster. "Time to market" became the rallying cry; product development time lines were compressed, and it became trendy to take a "ready, fire, aim" approach. One way that corporate leaders justified this quest for speed was to point to the multibillion-dollar investments in IT equipment and services that were made in the 1990s. The new PCs and corporate networks were supposed to boost productivity and profits, and would, in fact, *allow* their companies to "do more with less."

This was true. But another truth got buried under the technology sales pitches. Achieving those gains would happen *only* after a significant initial investment in training and in "system integration" to make sure that all the pieces meshed well with each other. This goal was made more difficult to achieve due to the problem referred to by many as "paving over the cowpaths."

Trying to modernize a city by paving the dirt roads with blacktop doesn't help much if all you do is pave the existing twisted maze of narrow paths suitable for horses and cattle but not for cars and buses. Similarly, pouring thousands of PCs and miles of cables into a corporation was a great way to waste money unless the systems and processes that technology was meant to automate were overhauled—in other words, the corporate "cowpaths" were straightened and widened before being paved over with all those chip-laden wonders. Unfortunately, this all became somewhat irrelevant. The expectation was that more technology meant more speed and more output per employee—and when those results didn't always magically occur, the only way to produce them was to require people to work longer hours.

Oddly, the same thing happened even when the technology delivered as promised. Consider the case of presentation software such as Microsoft's PowerPoint, which has become a corporate staple. Before PowerPoint, a graphics presentation would have to be created by a graphic artist using highly complex software or even something less sophisticated and more manual in nature. With PowerPoint and its software cousins, just about anyone could sit down at a PC and, without much training or practice, produce an on-screen presentation or a slick set of slides, handouts, or transparencies that looked fully professional.

On one hand, this software actually *was* a productivity tool—it took only hours to do what might have taken days previously, and the result was just as good—if not better. But it didn't stop there. Once everyone saw how easy it was to use these programs, they were used more and more. Thus, a senior manager who wouldn't have considered asking an analyst to spend a couple of days working up a slide presentation using Stone Age technology didn't hesitate to direct the same analyst to prepare that presentation using the desktop PC and PowerPoint. The goal was for this analyst to *save* time by using the software; the likely outcome was that he or she spent *more* time on presentations and had less time available for other aspects of the job.

The Employer Bottom Line

These three forces—downsizing, globalization, and the need for speed—combined to change the work environment from being comfortably busy to being a nonstop workshop in which most people felt they could never get caught up and could never stop to take a breather.

My point is not that employers should have ignored these forces; those who did flirted with disaster. Like it or not, the pace and pressures in organizations did heat up in the last decade and especially in the late 1990s. We are still seeing the effects of those changes on the everyday schedules of most office workers.

Where Do We Go Next—and *Is* the Grass Greener Elsewhere?

Now you have the "big picture" background about why so many people seem to be working for so long in so many places. The three contributing factors were shown in a triangle earlier because they are inseparable; we can't affect one without affecting at least one of the other two. That's why we'll focus on all three as the rest of the book gives you methods for redrawing some boundaries in your life.

Maybe you're starting to think that the most expedient way to deal with these issues is to move beyond them, instead of working on a plan to cope with and improve them where you are now. You might be especially tempted to look elsewhere if you're in a situation with your employer or your clients that simply breeds pressure, tight deadlines, and nonstop work. If you're thinking that things might be better elsewhere, and that it's time to polish up your resumé so you can find a job where it doesn't seem you're working 23 hours out of every 24, I'm afraid I have some bad news. The grass really isn't much greener anywhere else—or at least, not a whole lot greener.

To be sure, some employers face more pressure than others; their customers, competition, and technology might be different, they might be growing faster, or they might be getting ready for an IPO. In most cases, though, you'll find that the three underlying factors described here are more universal and widespread than you think. That's not to say that some employers or clients aren't pure stress factories—but havens from some stress are less common than you might like to imagine.

Before you take my word for it, there's something you can do to determine how typical or atypical your situation is: *look* around and *ask* around. Next time you're on a business trip and you see someone working in the airport or on a plane, ask that person about his or her workweek. Talk to your friends and neighbors about their jobs. Observe how full the parking lots are at other offices as you drive past them on the way home from your office. Chances are you'll find that your situation isn't all that unusual.

If that's true, then jumping ship can actually make your situation *more* difficult and *more* stressful, and not less. A new hire is always under more pressure to produce and to convince management that their hiring decision was right. When you have some tenure with your current employer, you have a bit more leverage and a bit more cushioning against the stresses and strains of everyday workloads.

It may well be that your best career move *is* to look for a new position—but if you do, make sure you're doing the right thing for the right reason. It's probably unrealistic to expect that your workload or work hours will be dramatically reduced as long as you want to stay at your same income level. If you like your current job in all aspects other than the long hours and permeable boundaries between work and the rest of your life, follow the advice in this book to try to fix that situation first. If the problems continue, *then* it's probably time to look for those greener pastures.

These New Problems Have Old Roots

We ended the last decade (and century, and millennium) with the sense that everything was going faster, that we were being tugged in too many directions, and there was never enough time to do what we wanted. Now we've seen how the combination of changes in technology, employers, and employees collude to create these pressures. In many ways, these forces seem to be purely a product of the last half of the 1990s.

While the pace of change might have speeded up in the last few years, at least one observer noted that these transitions had earlier roots. Here are some thought-provoking excerpts from a December 31, 1989, *New York Times* editorial titled, simply, "Faster" with the subtitle "The 1980's: When Information Accelerated":

> Not so long ago, citizens could depend on a letter arriving anywhere in the country in four days, or two days by air mail. They could count on taking a day or two to respond in a careful, stately fashion. A few days after that, their answer would be received . . . Careful and stately mail has gone the way of attractive handwriting: both endure mainly in the world of wedding invitations. The phone is faster.

And getting faster still. For one thing, there are twice as many phones as there were 20 years ago. For another, it's harder to escape the phone, even in the bathroom. They are now, commonly, cordless and portable. Indeed, in this cellular age, they can be found almost anywhere, including the family car.

The printed word moves far more quickly, too. In 1970, the fax machine was largely a curiosity. Today, there are six million, speeding whole documents across continents and oceans. And the modem is faster still. The computer business, having transformed industry through mainframes, is itself being transformed by the personal computer, which confers upon ordinary mortals the power to compose reports and graphics that, presto, can be sent instantly elsewhere.

Those awestruck words with which the *Times* described the 1980s sound absolutely ancient today. Hearing someone marvel at the wonders of the cell phone or the fax machine seems almost laughable at a time when we have digital video cameras that fit in a shirt pocket, fax machines on a chip, and direct-broadcast satellite TV, among others.

You experienced the pace at which our technologies—and our expectations about using them—accelerated in the decade of the 1990s, so you can imagine what the first decade of this new century might hold. Or perhaps you can't—perhaps we are all so overwhelmed by the deluge of technological developments that we just can't conceive of what lies beyond the bend. If the *Times* had updated that editorial for December 31, 1999, maybe it might have been titled "Even Faster Yet."

That's precisely why it's time to take a breather from this exhilarating but exhausting pace.

Smash All the Machines? No Way!

While you might have the urge at times to toss your pager into the river, or "accidentally" pour a can of soda on the keyboard of your laptop, you can't make those tools—and the work you do with them—go away that easily.

This book isn't intended to stir up a revolution against today's portable technology. Instead, it's meant to help you *use and deal with* that technology more effectively in three ways:

- *Understand* the role that mobile-office tools and technology play in your life, and determine whether they might be hurting as much as helping.
- *Decide* how and where you want to begin drawing the line between the part of your life that you're willing to devote to anytime-anywhere work, and the rest of your life that you'd rather reserve for yourself.
- *Develop* a customized plan for regaining control of your use of these tools, and then discussing your plan and its implications with your clients, manager, and co-workers—in a way that will gain their cooperation.

I can't promise that you'll go from a 60- or 70-hour workweek down to a 40-hour week; after all, that might have gone the way of the rotary telephone. We seem to be committed to a world of work in which "Do more with less—and do it faster" is the guiding principle. Nevertheless, that doesn't mean the nonstop work made possible by today's technology is really beneficial over the long term for you or your customers, clients, or employer.

To find out how to cope effectively with these workload issues, here's what you'll learn in the following chapters:

Self-Assessment (Chapters 2 and 3): How badly *you* need to "turn it off"—and how you can find a solution;

The "Three Zones" Model (Chapter 4): How to think about the workweek in a new way, by dividing up the 168 hours of each week into three zones that vary according to how much you're willing and available to be "on duty";

Developing Your Plan (Chapter 5): How to use the "Three Zones" model to make some conscious, deliberate decisions about dividing your days and weeks into periods of time when you're completely *on* the job, completely *off* the job, and somewhere in between;

Communicating Your Plan (Chapter 6): How to find the best (and safest) ways to approach your boss, clients, or co-workers to let them know how you want to change the way you make yourself available to them—without jeopardizing your job or your relationships;

The Manager's Role (Chapter 7): How to put these principles into action if *you* are the boss and you want to be sure that your staff meets your needs for getting the work done and their needs for having a life;

The Future (Chapter 8): How this phenomenon of anytime-anywhere work—and our ability to cope with it—is likely to evolve in the near future, why it could have crucial implications for all employers, and how likely it is that *you'll* be able to "turn it off"';

What to Do if All Else Fails (Chapter 9): What to do if you just can't seem to "turn it off" no matter what you do— and how you can try to retain some semblance of sanity amid your laptops, phones, cables, and power cords.

Whether you're a self-employed business owner, a "road warrior," an employee who takes work home at night, a telecommuter or teleworker who works at home during the day, or someone who manages or works with any of them, this book is your key to finding the right balance between all the things you *need* to do to earn a living and all the things you *want* to do to have a life.

CHAPTER 2

How to Find Out if You've
Gone over the Line

How is your own life affected by the anytime-anywhere work world? It may not be realistic for most of us to cut back to only 35 or 40 work hours a week, but it *is* realistic to set some limits as to how far beyond those numbers we stretch the week. More important, it's realistic to draw some boundaries around the number of places at which we do our work away from the office.

By the end of this chapter you'll have more insight into your own work habits. Let's start that process by learning about specific sources of nonstop-work pressures.

The reason for starting with this kind of analysis is to let you determine the extent to which you actually experience these kinds of boundary-setting problems. As you'll see throughout the book, I've tried to put this decision in your hands rather than prescribing a "one best answer" solution.

How Often Is "Often"? How Soon Is "Soon"?

We can all agree that it's good business practice to check voice mail and e-mail messages often—and to respond to those messages soon. But "often" and "soon" are two notoriously slippery words; you may check your voice mail every 30 minutes and I may check mine every two hours, and we both feel we're checking it "often enough." You may respond to your messages immediately and I may wait as long as a few hours (unless a message is clearly urgent), and once again, we both feel we're responding "soon enough."

To better understand how our different interpretations of the simple words "often" and "soon" play a role in stretching the boundary of the workday, consider the questions below. Don't overanalyze these simple questions—don't worry about time-zone differences, whether you're working on a superurgent project, whether it's your boss versus a co-worker, and so on. Just think about the general situation—there will always be exceptions but for now, focus on what you feel to be standard and normal.

Also, don't be concerned—yet—with how you *feel* about having to respond to those messages by a certain time. We're only trying to establish a baseline about what has become normal for you *whether or not* you mind receiving and having to respond to those messages.

- If someone with whom you work fairly closely and frequently sent you an e-mail or voice mail message at 6 P.M. on a Tuesday, by what day and time would you feel you had to reply to it?
- If someone with whom you work fairly closely and fre-

quently sent you an e-mail or voice mail message at 6 P.M. on a Friday, by what day and time would you feel you had to reply to it?

- What if that message was sent at 8 P.M. on a Tuesday? At 8 P.M. on a Friday? And to make it more interesting, what if the message was sent at 8 A.M. on Saturday morning— by what day and time would you feel you had to reply under *those* conditions?

Your answers to these questions are a simple but not simplistic proxy measure of the extent to which the demands on your time may have stretched beyond where you'd like them to be. The shorter the interval between the time a message is sent and the time we're expected to respond, the more pressure we feel from that aspect of our jobs. Similarly, if that interval really isn't much different whether the message comes in during the weekday, during the evening, or on a weekend day, it's likely that you are feeling you can never get away from those electronic demands on your time.

How the Response Times Got Compressed

My view is that the length of the allowable "response gap" began to shorten when two business tools we now take for granted became well established in most offices: overnight package deliveries and fax machines. In both cases, the early users benefited from the novelty factor—"Wow—I just got an overnight package! This must be something *really* important— I'm going to drop everything and open it *now*!" Similarly, fax machines let us send a memo or report in a matter of seconds or minutes; an overnight package delivery was quicker than most people ever received printed materials previously, but a fax was unbelievably fast and almost instantaneous.

As good as these tools were, and are, they led to a confusion between the *means of delivery* and the desired *outcome*. Just because you could send a report to arrive across the country the next morning—or send a fax to arrive across an ocean in minutes—the sender seemed to expect that the receiver would drop everything and reply with equal speed.

We confused speed of delivery with speed of action. If I sent you a fax requesting an answer and it arrived at 3:00 P.M., I might have picked up the phone and called you if I didn't get your answer by 3:15 P.M. Never mind how much other work is on your desk, you just got an instant fax so you'd better reply *right now.*

The same kind of rapid-response thinking began to pervade the other ways we communicate. In the old days (way back in, say, 1981), a phone message that came in at 6 P.M. on Tuesday night would generally remain unanswered until you arrived in the office the next morning. In the rare case when someone would leave you a message at 8 A.M. on Saturday morning, it would almost always wait until Monday morning for an answer.

But today, many people have lost that distinction between workday and evening, and workweek and weekend. We are expected to respond almost as quickly even if that call comes when most people would be relaxing and thinking about anything but work. This is one reason why it has become harder to preserve time as personal time. You'll learn more in Chapter 5 about ways to reestablish some boundaries in your life so you can get a well-deserved break.

Mapping Your Mobility

To see how extensively your own office work has moved beyond the office walls, take a few minutes to fill out this "work on the run" survey. No one else will see the results, so be honest about *all* the places where you do your work—especially as you get to the bottom of the list. This won't take long, and it will give you insight into the work and work location patterns that make up your weeks.

INSTRUCTIONS: For each work location, write down your time "score" using the scoring key. This is the amount of time you spent doing job-related work last week (or in a typical seven-day week) at this location.

Then, go back over the list and decide at which locations you were networked or "networkable" in any way—you used a laptop, a wired or wireless phone, a PDA, or any other device that was connected to the telephone network (and/or to the Internet or to your corporate network) or could have been. For these locations, *double* your score from the first column and write it in the second column:

Scoring Key

Time Last Week	Score
0–15 minutes	0
15 minutes–1 hour	1
1–3 hours	2
3–5 hours	3
Over 5 hours	4

Location	Score for Time Spent Last Week	Double Score if Networked
A. In your office building		
Your assigned desk/cubicle	_____	_____
Someone else's assigned desk/cubicle	_____	_____
A hoteling or drop-in space	_____	_____
Conference room	_____	_____
Cafeteria	_____	_____
Other location	_____	_____
B. In your home		
Your home office	_____	_____
Elsewhere at home	_____	_____
C. In transit *for business purposes*		
Airplane/airport	_____	_____
Train/train station	_____	_____
Bus	_____	_____
Subway	_____	_____
Car or other vehicle	_____	_____
Hotel/motel (business travel)	_____	_____
D. Other business sites		
Client's office	_____	_____
Competitor's office	_____	_____
Alliance/partner office	_____	_____
Restaurant (business-related)	_____	_____
E. Other locations *not primarily business-related*		
Hotel/motel (personal travel)	_____	_____

Location	Score for Time Spent Last Week	Double Score if Networked
Vacation home	_____	_____
Restaurant	_____	_____
Airplane/Airport	_____	_____
Sports stadium	_____	_____
Entertainment/cultural site	_____	_____
Children's game/concert/play	_____	_____
Beach/lake/park or other outdoors	_____	_____
Other	_____	_____
TOTAL	_____	_____

If you add up both columns, you'll get totals between 30 and 80 in the first column, and as high as double that range for the second column. There are no correct answers; the purpose of this exercise is to show you three things:

- The *variety of locations* where you did job-related work last week
- The *fragmented nature* of your workweek
- A rough measure of the effect of *networking technology* on your location pattern

Here are some issues to consider to help you interpret your scores.

1. Multisite Chaos. For some people, there is something comforting about the predictability of going to the same

office day after day and doing most of their work there. These people would find it chaotic and stressful to spread their work across five, ten, or more different locations such as those indicated above. For others who thrive on variety and mobility, it would be a true curse to sit in the same office every day.

Consider where you are on that spectrum of single-site versus multisite locations, and compare your answer with the number of locations you identified in the first column. If you treasure predictability and a more routine schedule, a high number of locations—apart from any measure of the number of hours you work at each—could be a source of stress. You may or may not be able to control that, but if you can you'll be able to change your workweek so you feel less harried.

2. Short-Interval Scheduling. This relates to the *number* of locations at which you do your work: it's the *amount of time* spent at each. Once again, different people have different tolerances for working in short bursts of activity versus being able to settle down and settle in to work on a task to completion. If you thrive on those short bursts, and they don't interfere with your ability to get your work done, then a high number of locations coupled with a short duration of time spent at many of them may not be a problem. But if you're the type who values having longer periods of time (with few or no interruptions) then you might consider how you can adjust your work patterns—even if it means carving out some time from what otherwise might be personal time.

3. The Joy Versus the Pains of Being Wired. Look at the second column. If you have lots of items with those doubled scores, it indicates that you are truly the mobile-networked

worker. That's fine if you get a thrill out of being able to check your e-mail while sitting in a taxi or uploading a report via cellular modem after working over lunch in a restaurant.

Wireless connection speeds are almost always lower—sometimes significantly so—than with a wired connection, and in fact the ability to make and maintain a good wireless connection isn't assured. Even with a wired connection (such as plugging a phone line from your laptop's modem into a data port in an airport or hotel telephone), your access speeds are almost always slower than if you are wired into the network in your office.

Depending on the nature of your work, you may be able to simplify your work life and squeeze out some of the stress by sacrificing the "work anywhere" ability with wireless or wired public-access connections in favor of waiting until you're back in the office, in your home office, or somewhere else where you have a faster and more reliable connection.

Note that the speed and ease-of-connection penalty most people pay for working on the go is starting to disappear. It's safe to say that a wired connection will almost always be faster and more reliable than a wireless one, but the wireless (and public-access) connections are catching up quickly. The same advanced telecommunications technologies that affect how we work in the office are spreading to other locations.

If you're so inclined, you can do lots more analysis on your scores—the percentage of time spent in your office versus elsewhere, or the different effect of technology across different work locations. No matter what your scores were, it's safe to say that they are considerably higher in both columns than they would have been five or ten years ago, *and* there's a bigger difference between the scores in the two columns than would have existed five or ten years ago. We're working in more places and in more "non-work" locations, and with more technology in hand, than ever before.

Keep in mind that the problem is *not* simply the number of hours you work, or the number of places in which you do the work. The inescapable reality is that almost everyone today is working more hours than they did in the past and in more places than in the past. The laptops, cell phones, PDAs, ubiquitous Internet access and all the rest really are liberating technologies and I wouldn't give them up for anything. Our challenge is to make sure that we really are being liberated, not enslaved or frustrated, by all those tools.

The Techno-Mobile Resentment Scale

Just as the "Mapping Your Mobility" exercise helped you understand how much and in how many places you are working, the following scale will shed some light on how this is affecting you and those around you. I don't claim this to be a scientifically validated scale, but the positive feedback from colleagues, conference audiences, and clients in a wide variety of *Fortune* 500–size corporations who have tried it indicates that it's a useful way to begin to understand these issues.

INSTRUCTIONS: For each of the following 20 questions, choose one of these four answers to describe how you or your significant others feel in response to the topic question (No doubt you know how *you* feel about each item—though it may help to take a moment to reflect carefully before answering—but you may have to make some educated guesses about how your significant others feel, unless they have explicitly told you.) Do you:

- Accept it;
- Tolerate it;
- Resent it;
- Hate it?

Note: If you think a question does not apply to you, you have two choices: you can score it 1, which means that there is no resentment attached to this question for you or anyone else. For example, look at Item P: if you live alone and don't have any roommates, family, or friends who would notice (let alone be affected by) your working at home at night, then there isn't any problem for anyone else.

Alternatively, look at Item C: if you spend no time at all working in a home office and the reason is that your employer won't allow you to or you don't have suitable technology to do so, then your answer might be 3 or even 4 because you resent *not* being able to work at home after hours.

Please be sure to score *every* item with one of the four choices, and don't leave any of them blank.

A. How you feel about the total number of hours you spend in an average week working in *your* office (wherever that is): _____

B. How you feel about the total number of hours you spend in an average week working in *someone else's* office (wherever that is): _____

C. How you feel about the total number of hours you spend in an average week working in your *home office:* _____

D. How you feel about the total number of hours you spend in an average week working in your home but *not* in a home office: _____

E. How you feel about the total number of hours you spend in an average week working *in transit* (in a car, bus, plane, train, subway): _____

F. How you feel about the total number of hours you spend in an average week working before or after what *you* would consider "normal business hours" during the standard Monday through Friday workweek: _____

G. How you feel about the number of times you are implicitly or explicitly expected to check and respond to voice mail or e-mail before or after what *you* would consider "normal business hours" during the standard Monday through Friday workweek: _____

H. How you feel about the number of times you are paged and are implicitly or explicitly expected to respond to that page before or after what *you* would consider "normal business hours" during the standard Monday through Friday workweek: _____

I. How you feel about the total amount of time you spend in an average week working before or after what *you* would consider "normal business hours" on a Saturday or Sunday:

_____

J. How you feel about the total amount of time you spend in an average week working during what *you* would consider "normal business hours" on a Saturday or Sunday:

_____

K. How you feel about the number of times you are implicitly or explicitly expected to check and respond to voice mail or e-mail on a Saturday or Sunday: _____

L. How you feel about the number of times you are paged and are implicitly or explicitly expected to respond to that page on a Saturday or Sunday: _____

M. How you feel about the amount of time you have spent (in the last six months) working on a paid holiday (not including during vacation periods): _____

N. How you feel about the amount of time you have spent (in the last six months) working on a paid vacation period of one full day or longer: _____

Note: For the items that follow unless otherwise stated, you can define "family" however you like for the remaining questions. It can be your roommate(s), spouse, or significant other and/or children and/or parents and other relatives, whether or not these people live with you. While the effects of your work schedule and work habits will be most noticeable to those living under your roof, others with whom you have ongoing relationships may also be affected.

O. All things considered, the way your family feels about your work schedule and work habits: _____

P. The way your family feels about your work schedule and work habits in the evening during the normal workweek:

_____

Q. The way your family feels about your work schedule and work habits on Saturdays and Sundays: _____

R. The way your family feels about your work schedule and

work habits while you are on vacation with some or all of them: _____

S. The way your child(ren) feel about the extent to which you are able to spend time with them in the evening during the normal workweek: _____

T. The way your child(ren) feel about the extent to which you are able to spend time with them on Saturdays and Sundays: _____

SCORING: Add up the number of 1s, 2s, 3s, and 4s you chose for your answers and write them in Column 1; when you're done, Column 1 should total 20:

	Column 1	Column 2	Column 3
number of 1s	_____	× 1 =	_____
number of 2s	_____	× 2 =	_____
number of 3s	_____	× 3 =	_____
number of 4s	_____	× 4 =	_____
		Grand Total	_____

Then multiply the counts in Column 1 by the scores in Column 2, and write the answers in Column 3. Last, add up Column 3 for your Grand Total.

Interpreting Your Scores

Keep in mind that this exercise does not measure the number of hours or places you work, but rather your (and your significant others') *feelings about* those hours and places. This is an important distinction: the premise of this book is to help you determine how satisfied you are with your work patterns and make changes if needed—not to *assume* that you are working too many hours in too many places and that you must reduce both.

1. Liking It or Living with It. Look in Column 1 at the number of items you scored with each of the four answer choices. The more 1s and 2s you have the more you and your significant others can accept, or at least tolerate, your work patterns. As you start to build up more 3s and 4s, that's a clear signal that something is not right.

Go back to the list of 20 items and circle the ones that you scored with a 3 or 4 and see what pattern exists among them. Do they all refer to after-hours work during the workweek, or work on weekends, on vacations and holidays, or some other pattern?

2. Who Is Resentful? Items A–N measure your own feelings about your work patterns, while Items O–T measure your estimate of the feelings of those around you. Do you see any clear patterns or differences between the scores for those two groups of items? If *you* accept or at least tolerate your patterns but your significant others don't, your motivation to change might not be as high as if both you *and* they are resentful.

It's also possible that you scored your own resentment higher than you projected for your significant others. Maybe that means they're just as happy whether or not you are out of the house and not involved in household or family activities. You might view this pattern as meaning that it's only your own stress that you must be concerned with (and that's very possible).

There are two other interpretations, both of which could

be more troubling. It could be that your significant others have become immune to your long hours and the intrusion of your work into personal time. Or, it could be that the long hours and near-nonstop work have taken their toll on them indirectly because of how those stresses affect how you deal with them.

For example, maybe you feel you can't ever get much of a break from work and that causes you to be upset and short-tempered with them if you're asked to participate in a household activity instead. If that's true, maybe they would just as soon have you do your work. If you project—even unwittingly—that your commitments to and involvement with your significant others are unwelcome interruptions of your work, it won't take long for most family and friends to simply withdraw from relationships with you.

This book isn't about marriage or family counseling, and if your scores for the resentment of others are high it doesn't mean you need that kind of counseling. However, scores and patterns of scores that suggest possible family frictions should be a red flag to you to at least consider the unintended consequences of your work.

3. Your Telling Total. Finally, let's look at the Grand Total score. Assuming you left no questions blank, your total score for the 20 questions can range from 20 (20 questions all scored 1) to 80 (20 questions all scored 4). The lower the Grand Total, the less resentment you experience yourself or perceive that your significant others feel about your work patterns.

Because more weight is given to the scores 3 and 4, a small change in the pattern of the answers can have a significant effect on the Grand Total. For example, look at these two possible sets of answers for Joe and Jane:

Joe's Scores:

number of 1s	2×1	$= 2$
number of 2s	5×2	$= 10$
number of 3s	7×3	$= 21$
number of 4s	6×4	$= 24$
GRAND TOTAL		$= 57$

Jane's Scores:

number of 1s	6×1	$= 6$
number of 2s	4×2	$= 8$
number of 3s	6×3	$= 18$
number of 4s	4×4	$= 16$
GRAND TOTAL		$= 48$

Jane's total is nine less than Joe's, though if you look at the patterns of their scores there doesn't appear to be much difference. A closer look reveals that Joe has 13 items scored 3 or 4 while Jane only has a total of 10 for those two scores.

That's the most detailed analysis we can do with these two examples, but you can go back to your own results and look at the breakdown of 1 and 2 scores versus higher scores as noted above, and also look at which items got the lowest and highest scores. Also, if your most recent job before your current one is still fresh in your mind, try scoring the questions again with that job in mind and see how the totals differ. That will give you some insight into understanding why you and your significant others might feel better—or worse—about your current position.

Getting Ready to Change

Now that you have a better understanding of where and when
you work, and how this affects you and those around you, it's
time to put this all together and list your own opportunities
for change and improvement. These will carry into the next
three chapters. You'll be referring to this chart as you go on,
so you might want to photocopy it so you can refer to it easily.
This chart will help you focus on the specific goals you have
about changes you need to make and benefits that will result
if you make those changes.

For each of the following questions, indicate with a check
mark whether your interest in tackling these issues is High,
Medium, or Low.

I need to:	*High Interest*	*Medium Interest*	*Low Interest*
1. Get out of my office earlier in the afternoon/evening	_____	_____	_____
2. Spend less time working with my computer at home in the evening	_____	_____	_____
3. Spend less time checking and answering voice mail at home in the evening	_____	_____	_____
4. Spend less time participating in conference calls at home in the evening	_____	_____	_____

I need to:	High Interest	Medium Interest	Low Interest
5. Spend less time responding to pages at home in the evening	_____	_____	_____
6. Spend less time working with my computer at home on weekends/holidays	_____	_____	_____
7. Spend less time checking/answering voice mail at home on weekends/holidays	_____	_____	_____
8. Spend less time participating in conference calls at home on weekends/holidays	_____	_____	_____
9. Spend less time responding to pages at home on weekends/holidays	_____	_____	_____
10. Spend less time working with my computer while on vacation	_____	_____	_____
11. Spend less time checking and answering voice mail while on vacation	_____	_____	_____
12. Spend less time participating in conference calls while on vacation	_____	_____	_____

I need to:	High Interest	Medium Interest	Low Interest
13. Spend less time responding to pages while on vacation	_____	_____	_____
14. Figure out how I want to spend my time and re-establish time boundaries	_____	_____	_____
15. Feel more confident/comfortable discussing these issues with my boss or clients	_____	_____	_____
16. Figure out how to take the risk out of discussing these issues with my boss	_____	_____	_____
17. Feel more confident/comfortable discussing these issues with my clients	_____	_____	_____
18. Feel more confident/comfortable discussing these issues with my co-workers	_____	_____	_____
19. Figure out what I'd do with extra time each week if I could find it	_____	_____	_____
20. Decide whether a change in jobs/careers would make it easier to control my time	_____	_____	_____

The items you marked as either Medium or High interest are the ones that should be foremost in your mind as you continue through the next three chapters. If you have more than ten items thus marked, you might go back and highlight the ones that are of most importance to you and that would give you the most value if improved. Having too many things to change can be immobilizing; you'll feel there's so much to do that it's impossible to get started, let alone do it all.

All This and Crankiness, Too?

You now have a firm grasp on the background factors and on their impact on you. As we move into the next chapters you'll learn how you can start tackling the challenges you face.

Before doing so, you might consider one last effect all of today's pressures have on us: many of us are becoming downright cranky, myself included at times. When my wife tells me I'm being cranky, that's one of my cues that I'm trying to do too much in too little time. I'm not alone, according to C. Leslie Charles, author of *Why Is Everyone So Cranky?: The Ten Trends That Are Making Us Angry and How We Can Find Peace of Mind Instead*. She lists ten trends that account for the moodiness and short tempers we see around us; the two at the top of the list are "Compressed Time—Feed the rush" and "Communication Overload—Too much, too often." (You can learn more about the book and her views on her Web site at <www.whyiseveryonesocranky.com>.)

I asked Leslie how this crankiness comes about, especially as it relates to our work. "We've become victims of the expectations machine when it comes to technology. We are led to believe that technology in all forms will make life easier, but in fact it has made life more complex for each of us," she said. "It has added layers of new work and new obligations to our existence.

"When this happens we start to question ourselves," she continued. "For example, if we can't get through 200 e-mail messages quickly we ask, 'What's wrong with me?' when we should really be asking, 'What's wrong with this technology?'"

She also believes that corporate commitments to nonstop service may be creating some unintended consequences. "The 24/7 philosophy means for many people that they have no time off, especially if this is the basis for the customer service the employer provides. The expectation is that the technology allows us to provide nonstop customer service—and just because it can, we should use it that way. What we don't realize is that not only does this make things difficult for the employee, but for the customer or client, too."

Commenting on the overall effect of our "do more with less" environment, she concluded as follows: "Corporate America continues to ask more and more of employees, even in the face of diminishing returns. It's true that managers and employers are getting more out of people by virtue of these mobile, round-the-clock technologies—but people are getting less out of life. Slowly, their careers are eroding their lives. Employees are being conditioned to believe that "first I have a career and *then* I have a life, if I'm lucky."

Not a pretty picture for some people, perhaps. But if that's how you're feeling at times, you can begin to get things back under control—and possibly be a little less cranky—by forging ahead to Chapter 3.

How You Can Get Back in Control—
if You Want To

This book is about understanding and trying to change the habits we've developed about when and where we work. Imagine, however, that instead of thinking about working long hours and toting laptops, we are thinking about some other personal habits or attributes that we want to change but find difficult to do so.

For example, think about (take your choice) smoking, weight, exercise, drinking, or any not-work-related issue. People who partake too much (or too little, in the case of exercise) certainly *know* that there are consequences to their actions, and they *know* all the reasons why they should try to change. But nothing happens until the day comes when they look in the mirror and say to themselves, "Enough! I've run out of excuses and rationalization and denial. It's time to start turning things around—as difficult as that may be."

Is It "Enough!" Time for You?

Based on your personal assessments from Chapter 2, you should now have a good idea of the extent to which your work is spilling over into your personal life in ways that you don't appreciate. Whether or not this is enough to motivate you to tackle this issue is your decision and yours alone. Don't be swayed by either the "kick back and enjoy life" or the "be a team player" voices that you might hear in your head, based on messages that have been implanted by friends, co-workers, bosses, or anyone else.

If you're concerned that taking action means taking big risks, you can relax. This book isn't intended to send you on a career suicide mission in which you storm into your boss's (or key client's) office, pound on the desk, and demand that you get your life and personal time back—or else. No matter how good the job market may be in your field, you can't count on having your boss drop everything and ask how he or she can make your life simpler and better in order to keep you on the payroll.

Similarly, the goal isn't to turn you into a modern-day Luddite* who takes a big hammer to the machinery of the Information Age office and smashes all the equipment that is the source of your frustration. That might be nice to imagine,

---

* Incidentally, if you're interested in the origins and outcomes of the Luddite movement, take a look at the fascinating "Ballad of Ned Ludd" site at <www.bigeastern.com/ludd/temp.htm> and the page of links on that site. The Luddites are often held up as models for why and how to rally against technology, but it's a bit more complicated than that.

but even if you did it the feeling of relief and satisfaction is likely to be short-lived. Worse, the underlying reasons *why* that phone is ringing and that laptop is feeding you e-mail won't have been tackled.

The Basic Premise for Change: It's Your Own Responsibility

By now you should be realizing that:

- The world, your boss, your clients, and everyone else around you aren't going away, so you have to learn to cope with (rather than hope to escape) the pressures they create;
- Mobile-office technology isn't a fad and is only going to become faster, smaller, better, and cheaper, so you can't pretend you can escape its influence;
- Your own desire to carve out some more free time in your life is valid and justified, but since no one is going to hand you a few more unencumbered hours each day, you'll have to work out a way to make better use of the hours, days, and weeks that you have.

That's the secret to regaining control of your time and your life—and that's the basis of the approach you'll use in the next two chapters. I simply do not believe that most managers and employers will recognize this anytime-anywhere work problem as something *they* need to act upon. A precious few have, and a few more will, but odds are that *your* employer isn't among them.

Unless you're willing to cut back to three hours of sleep each night and forego most of your vacation time, *you need to make some difficult but essential decisions about how available you want to be to your employer and your clients*, and how you can take responsibility for implementing those decisions.

Think about it: why *would* an employer arbitrarily decide to help its employees reestablish some reasonable boundaries between work and life? Leaving aside the long-term benefits (e.g., reduced stress, lower turnover), look at what is believed to be gained by employers who continue to stretch the workday and workweek:

- Same Salary—More Work. Each new hire costs employers not only salary but at least one-third more for benefits and entitlements—not to mention the costs of recruiting, relocation, training, and office space. If current employees are gently (or not so gently) encouraged to put in more hours, perhaps the employer can get by with fewer new hires—and see more dollars fall to the bottom line.
- Better Return on Investment. Look at all the equipment you have available at the office, in your briefcase, hooked onto your belt, and in your home office and car. Though all those boxes and gadgets represent a onetime capital expense, the return on that investment comes more quickly if they are used more often.
- Better Customer/Client Service. A mobile, wired, accessible workforce becomes a competitive edge when speed is everything as it is today. If you were a client or customer waiting for a response to your 5 P.M. inquiry, would you be more impressed with the firm that responds within an

hour or the one that responds by 9 A.M. the next morning? Note that it may not matter if there is actual business value in getting that response much more quickly—but it certainly *seems* like a faster answer is a more valuable answer.

My client who works for an international consulting firm commented on this last point: "We know that demands placed on our staff for immediate responses on a 24/7 basis are driven more by internal pressures than by direct client pressure. We also know that speed often doesn't equal quality. It seems that the old need for 'face time' has been replaced by the need for fast response time—and the irony is that neither is a good indicator of the quality of the work provided."

For these reasons, I am strongly convinced that anyone who wants to reestablish the boundaries needs to find a good way to do this on his or her own. Only a minority of employers will be insightful enough, concerned enough, or smart enough to take initiative on this issue.

"Smart Enough"?

That last sentence wasn't meant to imply that employers (or managers) are, on the whole, stupid. Instead, it means that employers differ in their ability to grasp the opportunities that are disguised as problems. The single most important reason why an employer should face these boundary issues is to preserve the quality of work produced by key employees— and, to go farther, keep those good workers on the payroll. Employers who can look beyond what appear to be the short-term benefits of extending the workday and the office into employees' personal time and space will gain more in the long run.

Here are three reasons why it pays for smart employers to rein in the anytime-anywhere office:

1. Employees Burn Out Today and Walk Out Tomorrow. Put yourself in the shoes of a competent, experienced employee in today's job market—for that matter, put yourself in your *own* shoes. How long will this person tolerate increasingly demanding expectations to be available and online in hours and places that previously were considered off-limits to the employer? The short-term gain of having responsive, available, accessible employees may create the long-term pain of watching those same people walk out the door in search of a more reasonable work schedule. While the grass might not always be greener elsewhere, an employee facing these kinds of pressures is certainly tempted to at least look for other choices.

There's another factor to consider. In today's downsized environment, the old adage "If you want something done, find a busy person to do it" seems to be applied more often than ever. A manager with limited resources and an almost unlimited workload can't help but turn to his or her most competent employees when there's more work to do. Managers assume (often incorrectly) that competence is a spongelike quality, and the employee who is doing a lot already will somehow be able to absorb just a little more. Thus, managers end up adding the insult of yet more work to the injury of an already overloaded to-do list, which results in even longer hours, more work crammed into weekends, vacations that are anything but, and a cumulative pressure that can push someone to the breaking point—and out the door.

2. The Snowball Effect of Turnover. When a mediocre employee leaves, almost nobody notices because that person's contribution was so minimal that its loss has few consequences. But when a top-notch employee leaves, the opposite happens: since a good worker is generally carrying *more* than his or her share of the workload, that burden falls immediately on everyone else, at least in the interim while a replacement is hired and trained.

Employees who are already likely to be kept busy by their own work now have to pick up some of what was being done by the departed superstar. This, in turn, can push the remaining staff close to or over their own limits, and cause *them* to start wondering if they should be looking for the greener pastures that their former co-worker sought and found. This cumulative effect of turnover is often not realized by management until it has taken its toll—and by that time it's too late to do much about it.

3. Nonstop Work Is Self-Defeating. Last and perhaps most elusive is the problem that few employers are willing to admit and fewer managers are ready to accept. The purpose of a two-day weekend, paid holidays, and paid vacation time is very simple: employees need a break; they need time to rest and recharge, and they need time to nurture and develop the non-work aspects of their lives. In the agricultural and factory eras, when work was much more physically demanding than it generally is today, these rest periods were necessary to maintain the employees' physical health. Today, these same breaks are necessary to maintain employees' *mental* health—

which, if taxed, can and often does result in physical woes as well.

In my view, the greatest irony about the trend toward extended work hours and work locations is that employers are likely to *lose* more performance, quality, and productivity in the long run than they will gain. The laptop-toting, pager-reading, voice-mail-answering weekend or vacation worker is likely to return from those intended break periods feeling *less* energized and *less* capable than he or she did beforehand. The very tools and technologies that appear in the short run to boost performance may well have the opposite effect, because the employee will face each new week feeling just as tired if not more so and perhaps even resentful that he or she never got a chance to get completely unplugged from the office.*

What About Your *Own* Selfish Interest?

Having just made the case for why employers should be motivated to change, let's now turn to something much more relevant to you: what you'll gain if you change and what you might lose if you don't.

It should be fairly obvious why you'd be interested in cre-

---

* The comments above about the effects on employers are not, of course, irrelevant to you. If you are a manager, you can take those messages to heart, and if you're not, you can use them to help make *your* case with your manager. You'll learn more about that in Chapter 6.

ating a little more breathing room in your life by squeezing out some of the work intrusions. You probably have a long mental list of the things you don't get to do, or would like to start doing, if you just had a bit more control over your time and a bit less of a feeling of being "on call" for so many hours and in so many places.

I think it's valuable to move that mental list onto paper for two reasons. First, it makes you more conscious of what you'd like to do differently; second, seeing your own words on paper is the beginning of your own personal contract with yourself—a contract that will help commit you to the course of change that you'll be forging in Chapter 5.

For these reasons, take a few minutes—*now*—to respond to the six questions below. Try first to write down what comes to mind most quickly; this will capture what's most important to you. Then take a few minutes to think more deeply about these questions, because it's possible that you've worked in the anytime-anywhere mode for so long that you've subconsciously suppressed your own "wish lists" because what you want seemed unattainable. Let those thoughts bubble back up to the surface and see if you can fill in all five lines for each of these six questions:

1. If I could reduce the length of my typical workday by having more free time after normal working hours, I'd use that time to:

a. _____

b. _____

c. _____

d. _____

e. _____

2. If I could reduce the amount of work I normally do on the weekend, I'd use that time to:

a. _____

b. _____

c. _____

d. _____

e. _____

3. If I knew that I wouldn't have to check my e-mail and/or voice mail and/or respond to pages while on vacation or holiday, I'd change the way I use that time off by:

a. _____

b. _____

c. _____

d. _____

e. _____

4. If I could draw some boundaries around the times when I'm expected to be working or available to others—and still remain fully committed to my job—the likely effect this would have on my own attitude and outlook would be:

a. _____

b. _____

c. _____

d. _____

e. _____

5. The books I'd like to read, hobbies I'd like to start or develop, places I'd like to visit, or experiences I'd like to have if I could free up some more time in the evening and on the weekend are:

a. _____

b. _____

c. _____

d. _____

e. _____

6. If I could draw some boundaries around the times when I'm expected to be working or available to others—and still remain fully committed to my job—the likely effect this would have on my relationship with my significant other(s) would be:

a. _____

b. _____

c. _____

d. _____

e. _____

The last step in this exercise is to go back and circle the one item in each of the six lists that is your top priority—the item that would represent the greatest value and best return on your investment in changing your work habits. These are your own "80–20" items; you'll probably get 80 percent of the value of changing from this one out of five (20 percent) of the items you listed for each of the six questions.

One last point under the heading of "selfish interest"— your own health. The kinds of time pressures most of us face today can be stressful enough to affect not only our mental well-being but also our physical well-being. This was evident in a report issued in February 2000 by the Canadian Heart and Stroke Foundation—and its findings are certainly not limited to Canada. "Time pressures appear to be the prime contributing factor to high stress levels faced by Canadians today," the report stated. "There simply aren't enough hours in the day for most Canadians to accomplish all they want and need to do," said Dr. Rob Nolan, foundation spokesperson and stress expert. "Over half—53 percent—of our national sample reported that they don't have enough time for their family, friends or partners, or to do the things they want to do. Not only do time pressures squeeze out many of the joys in life, but they can also impact our heart health."

That wasn't meant to frighten you, but if it gave you cause to pause and consider some of these possibly very significant effects on your health, that's good enough. Work and careers are important, but I think we'd all agree that our health is even more important.

An Additional Observation for Parents

I hope that by now you've become more clear and convinced about the ways in which your anytime-anywhere work habits might be creating some problems for you, your employer, your customers, and your significant others. If you still need help getting off the fence and getting committed to making a change, here's one more attempt at explaining why a new outlook might make sense.

I have always been perplexed when I see parents who smoke and tell their kids not to, become couch potatoes and tell their kids to go out and get some exercise, twist the facts and tell their kids to always tell the truth, or imbibe far beyond the level of "social drinking" and tell their kids to stay away from drugs. That's why it was particularly amusing for me to read a March 3, 2000, *New York Times* article titled "Nothing Left to Buy? Pondering the Indiscreet Charm of the Super-rich," which included this quote from a partner, who will remain nameless here, at a California venture capital firm:

> [The partner] has made a lot more money than he had ever expected. But even among the circle he associates with, things are getting a little out of hand. "My 6-year-old is starting to say things like, 'their house is bigger,' [the partner] said, recalling a recent drive through his neighborhood in Menlo Park, Calif., in the heart of Silicon Valley. "She knows the different cars. It is troubling to me."

Why these observations from young children are revelations to today's parents is beyond me. Parents of today's adults who were baby-boomers might have been able to get away with a "Do as I say, not as I do" approach to role modeling and discipline, but *today's* parents simply can't pull that off. Today's kids—at every age from elementary school through college—are far too savvy and far less compliant than their parents and grandparents were.

If you want your children to have a life that is as good or better than yours is (and what parent doesn't?), you aren't helping matters by being visibly leashed to your job and your work. Just as the Silicon Valley father has perhaps unknowingly modeled "conspicuous consumption" for his child, workers who put in endless hours and steal work time from family time implant in their children's minds the notion that work is all-important. I would argue that no matter how justified that parent feels about doing office work on weekends, for example, the child learns that personal and family relationships come second in life, at best. I'm not sure that's the signal most parents want to send to their children.

True Confessions Time

The issue of the effect on children struck home—literally—for me when ours were in their preteen years and I had not yet realized the personal importance of finding the off switch on my computer and my work in general. My usual routine (on my in-the-home-office days) was to work through the day, come upstairs for dinner and be with the kids in the early evening, and then go back downstairs to my office for more work. I'd come up to say goodnight to them, often taking time to read with them, and then return to "the dungeon," as it became known.

The same kind of thing happened when we were on family vacations. Though I never toted the laptop—mostly because these mid-1980s years were before the e-mail deluge began—I would call in to check my answering machine at least once daily and try to return calls promptly. Many were the days that the family would be ready to leave the motel room and head off for whatever the day's venue was, and I'd be there on the phone signaling or silently mouthing "One more minute" as I tried to wrap up a call.

The last clue I had was what I call the "cost of not commuting," an odd phenomenon that many home-office workers share. The good news about not having to commute to and from an office each day is that you're spared the time, stress, and cost of the daily traffic wars. The bad news is that you also miss out on what is perhaps the single real benefit of the daily commute: having time in a buffer zone that separates your work from your life. That's important in the morning because it helps you get into the frame of mind to be ready to work when you arrive, but it is much more valuable at the end of the day because it lets you decompress and disengage before rejoining the rest of your life.

Since my commute consisted of a quick trip up a flight of stairs, I would often arrive at the dinner table (assuming it wasn't my day for kitchen duty) moments before we ate, having worked until the last possible minute. My body would be upstairs but my brain would still be downstairs—and this became evident to me because no one was including me in the dinner-table conversations. This wasn't the fault of my wife and kids—it was my fault because their past attempts to do so had been met with blank stares and unconvincing nods.

These indicators of my own failure to draw some boundaries convinced me (finally, my family would say) to think about my priorities, especially as I began to notice that the kids seemed reluctant to ask me for help or to play with them because they *assumed* I would be working or thinking about work. That in particular was my personal wake-up call, because I truly enjoyed the kids and didn't want to jeopardize our relationship. One of the real luxuries of having my own business and working from home is that I'd always been able to accompany them on class trips, attend school plays, be a baseball or soccer coach, and do many other things that more distant workers can't do as easily, which in turn can make them more distant parents.

My action plan was simple:

1. Later Is Better. If I needed to work in the evening, I'd put it off until after the kids were in bed, which was between 8 and 9 P.M., depending on their ages. As you may have surmised, this meant I would now risk ignoring my wife instead of our kids; that had its own set of problems but I felt that in the short term it was a good tradeoff. (Over time, those habits changed and I would either not work in the evening at all or keep it to a minimum—spouses of home-office workers can only be expected to endure so much.)

2. Work-Free Vacations. I decided to put my business on hold when we went on vacation—not at all an easy decision for a sole proprietor for whom not working means not having income. The first vacation during which I did not check messages daily was *not* the paragon of relaxation I'd thought it would be. I was nervous about missing that crucial call every entrepreneur imagines will transform him or her from a life of unpredictable struggles to a life of luxury. It took a couple of trips before I got the hang of it and realized that life would go on if I wasn't checking and responding to messages.

I'll go into more detail about this in Chapter 6, but let me say here that the key to pulling this off is giving early and detailed notification to clients, co-workers, and others who would reasonably expect to hear back from you if they called or sent e-mail. Not being able to reach me might have been frustrating for them (and financially painful for me), but *not knowing* that they wouldn't be able to reach me is much worse. To this day, I still agonize a bit about whether I'm missing that *one big call* while I'm away, but that worry is assuaged by the reinforcement I get from clients and colleagues who—when they hear my "I'm on vacation and not checking messages" voice mail announcement—leave a message saying, "Congratulations for taking a *real* vacation. I wish I could do the same thing!"

3. Creating an Artificial Commute. On the days when I'm working at home and am not on dinner duty, I always (well, *almost* always) stop working about 20 to 30 minutes before dinnertime and come upstairs. I'll sit down with the newspaper, perhaps with a glass of wine, and spend that time getting mentally disconnected from the work I left downstairs. By the time I join the family for dinner, I'm in a much better frame of mind—even if I don't have the wine—and ready to be as attentive and involved as I should be.

I didn't share this personal tale with you to convince you what a wonderful parent I am; besides, now that our kids have passed through their teenage years, they will tell you quite the opposite. I'm simply trying to illustrate how easy it is for all of us—parents or not—to drift into a style and schedule of working that insidiously robs us of much-needed time off.

What's more, it is incredibly easy for us to justify to ourselves (and others, if they're involved) why we're doing it. We tell ourselves, "I have a *really* important meeting tomorrow and I have to get ready," or "My boss is *expecting* to hear from me later tonight about this budget," and so on. The rationale and rationalizations are always there; the challenge is to slowly but surely put them into perspective and find a way to meet our obligations to our clients, employers, managers—*and* to ourselves.

It's possible to juggle what might seem to be conflicting demands as long as you've done the right analysis of your own time usage, decided on how to draw your boundaries, and communicated all that to those who rely on you. That's exactly what you'll be reading about in Chapters 4 through 6.

CHAPTER 4

THE "THREE ZONES" MODEL FOR BALANCING YOUR TIME AND WORK

Think of all the expressions we use to describe the passage of time: "Time flies," "The hours are dragging," "I don't know where the day went," and so on. When we're young, time seems to take forever to pass by—remember how *long* every day at school seemed? And as we get older, time starts to speed up; for most people the transition happens when they're in college, military service, or a similar post-adolescent transition. By the time we become senior citizens, a day might go in a flash and we simply can't imagine where the weeks and months have gone.

No matter how old we are, no matter what we're doing, and no matter what our personal situation, the immutable truth is that time is exactly the same for each of us. Every hour has 60 minutes, every day has 24 hours, and every week has seven days. No more, no less. It's how we use the time that counts.

We start each week with a balance-sheet credit of 168 hours and we end the week with 0 hours—and we have no control over how quickly that time disappears from the start of the week to the end. What we *can* control is how we choose to use those hours. An hour is a perishable commodity; once it has passed we can't recover it or change how we spent it. Rather than lament the passing of time or the effects of time choices imposed on us, it's much better to make deliberate choices about how we use our own time. By the time you finish this chapter and the next one, you'll have charted a very specific course for yourself and your time choices.

Time Management Without the "Management"

There are thousands of books about time management. Walk down the aisles of your local office-supplies store and you'll find dozens of calendars, scheduling systems, organizers, and other resources to help you plan your days. You can attend training seminars, buy cassette tapes, videotapes, and software, and learn from the time-management gurus. There's no lack of tips, tricks, and techniques to help you get your schedule and your time under control.

I have no quarrel with the various time-management authors, consultants, and experts, and readily admit to having benefited from the work of one of the earliest writers in that field, Alan Lakein, whose book *How to Get Control of Your Time and Your Life* (published in 1973 and updated since) features one of the best and most pragmatic approaches I've seen. But these time-management perspectives seem to fall short because they emphasize the management techniques without giving equal attention to what I believe is, in the context of this book, an equally important issue: your *fundamental right* to allocate some portion of your 168 weekly hours into "work-free" and "work-limited" zones.

This book isn't about becoming more efficient in how you handle your paperwork, or learning how to make your meetings more effective, or deciding how to prioritize that overwhelming to-do list you face every morning. Those are all important tasks, and they fall into the management-methods part of time management. If you aren't doing those and similar tasks well, you probably need to brush up on your skills to help you make the best use of your working hours—and there are thousands of books out there full of guidance on how to do so.

Instead, this book is about what you need to do *before* trying to become your own efficiency expert. Making the most out of your working hours is certainly important, but deciding *how many* working hours you want to have each week is, I would argue, much more important.

Understanding the "Three Zones" Model

If you're like most people, your days, nights, weekdays, and weekends have melted into one big pool of time. The traditional, and crystal-clear, distinctions between day and night, and between the workdays of the week and the non-workdays of the weekend, have probably become quite fuzzy and may have disappeared entirely. That's a natural consequence of the background factors discussed in Chapter 1 that lead to the extended work hours and the intrusions into what we'd normally think of as *non*-work times—including vacations.

As a result, you may be feeling that there are very few hours, let alone days, during which you aren't "on call" for work. That doesn't necessarily mean you're literally "on call" in the sense that a doctor might be, waiting for an unpredictable but urgent request for services. For most people, it means that you're feeling obligated—and perhaps required—to respond if you are paged or if someone calls you, and to take the initiative to check for incoming voice mail and e-mail.

Note that I am making the distinction here between the act of sitting down and doing work (e.g., drafting a report or analyzing a budget) and being electronically tethered to your job. The extent to which you have lots of work to do—which may require some time with the laptop in the evening or on the weekend—is certainly one source of intrusion into your otherwise personal time. But for most people, the most intrusive reach of the workplace comes from those electronic wonders—in particular, pagers, cell phones, and e-mail (via laptop or PDA). It is this kind of "reach out and find me" aspect of the workplace that can make it especially difficult for you to feel like you have some time of your own.

Most people are accustomed to thinking about their willingness to be available for work on a simple either-or scale—either I'm *on duty* at work and working, or I'm *off duty* and not at my workplace and not doing any work. Those are polar opposites that we can all understand and that let us divide our time quite simply. The problem is that an either-or choice doesn't help us deal with the gray areas in between—the times of day or days of the week when we're neither completely "on duty" nor "off duty"—and it is that middle ground we need to understand and explore. Those two extremes, plus the area between them, make up the three zones we'll be discussing.

A Trip to the Dry Cleaner

Let me explain how those zones work by using an entirely unrelated and, you might think, strange example: my local dry cleaner. As we look at the owner's choices and decisions about his hours of operation and services provided, you'll begin to see what choices and decisions lie ahead for you—even though you're probably not in the dry-cleaning business.

This establishment is open from 7 A.M. to 6 P.M. five days a week, Monday through Friday, and 8 A.M. to 5 P.M. on Saturday. If I bring in a suit to be dry-cleaned on, say, Tuesday morning before 10 A.M., I can pick it up at 5 P.M. the same day—and we'll call this the store's "on duty" time. If I try to bring in a suit at 10 A.M. on a Sunday morning, I'll find that the store is closed and thus it is "off duty" time. But if I bring in a suit on Saturday morning at 10 A.M., I won't be able to pick it up until *Monday* afternoon at 5 P.M.—even though the store is open almost the same hours on Saturday as on the previous five days of the week.

The reason is that the store operates with a smaller staff

(and on reduced hours) on Saturdays, and the dry-cleaning equipment is not running that day. This lets the store control its operating expenses (for labor, electricity, and supplies) but still serve its customers who might make a stop at the cleaner one of their normal Saturday errands. The store does not provide the *same* kind of service as it does Monday through Friday but provides *more* service than it does on Sunday. Thus, the store is open on Saturday—albeit for two fewer hours—but it's not *really* open in the sense that it is Monday through Friday. We might say that Saturday is the store's "mid-duty" time.

The purpose of this little side trip isn't to analyze the business practices of my local dry cleaner, or to have you decide whether or not you agree with the owner's decision about when and under what conditions he will be open. The purpose is to illustrate that he has, in fact, *made a deliberate decision* to create those three zones that divide up the seven-day week.

He could just as easily have decided to be open seven days a week and to provide full services for all seven days, but this would have cost him more in operating and salary expenses, and would also have intruded on his own free time and that of his staff. Or he could just as easily have decided to be open only five days a week, provide full service on those days, and close the store entirely on Saturday and Sunday. This choice would have trimmed his expenses considerably but also would risk alienating his customers and thus cost him business.

Here's how he might have weighed his options, based on the effect each had on his revenues, expenses, customer goodwill, and free time for himself and his staff:

Option	Effect on Revenues	Effect on Expenses	Effect on Goodwill	Free Time for Self/Staff
Open 7 days	Best	Worst	Best	Worst
Open 5 days	Worst	Best	Worst	Best
Open 6 days	Acceptable	Acceptable	Acceptable	Acceptable

By choosing to use Saturday as his "mid-duty" day, he apparently decided that while he might lose some revenue and some goodwill (by not being able to offer full service on Saturday), the tradeoff for doing so was to cut his expenses somewhat and provide more free time for himself and his staff.

(I didn't discuss all of this with the store owner, nor do I know that he went through this somewhat involved analysis. My guess, however, is that he put some thought into the choices and compromises and didn't come up with his schedule completely at random.)

From Suits and Pants to E-mail and Voice Mail

Moving back from the world of dry cleaning to your work world, let's understand and analyze the implications of this kind of decision making:

1. Time Is Not Necessarily Fungible. There it is—one of my favorite words, simply because I like the sound of it. But it also happens to perfectly describe the way most of us have

come to view time over the course of a day or week. The dictionary says that "fungible" is an adjective to describe "something that is exchangeable or substitutable," and it comes from the Latin *fungi*, meaning "to perform (in place of)." I noted earlier in this chapter that for most people today, our days, nights, weekdays, and weekends have melted into one big pool of time. This may seem to have some real benefits, but it also carries risks.

If we view time as fungible, it means that we rob ourselves of the distinctions that used to, and today still should, exist between day and night, and weekday and weekend—not to mention between work periods and holiday/vacation periods. Technology might make it possible to let us work at night at home *as if* we were working during the day in the office—but I don't think that means we should let those two time periods blend and merge completely.

Your first step in creating some zones of separation for yourself is to think about the extent to which you have slipped into this kind of boundaryless thinking about time. Unless you're the country's best neurosurgeon, or the person who carries the briefcase with the nuclear codes for your head of state, or the only person in your company who holds the physical or mental key to your trade secrets, there's no reason to feel you are *not* allowed or entitled to declare some of the 168 hours each week as off-limits and not fully "exchangeable or substitutable" for other time.

2. You *Do* Have Choices. My neighborhood dry cleaner has choices about his hours of operation. He makes those choices based on the factors noted above and also based on his view of what his competitors and other non-competing, but nearby, store owners are doing. Note that he chose to make Saturday

a very different day from the weekdays by reducing the hours *and* the services offered. It may not always be apparent to the outside observer, but those choices always exist.

I'm reminded of my father who owned and operated a small-town retail hardware store for more than 30 years—and he was in that store from 7:30 A.M. to 6 P.M. Monday through Saturday. When I was younger I could never understand why he kept those hours, and as a young child, probably resented the fact that he did. It wasn't until I was much older that I began to understand why he glued himself to that store: he was committed to "customer service" long before that term became as trendy as it is now.

He understood what it meant to be there at 7:30 in the morning so a local builder could pick up some nails he needed for a construction job that day, or to stay open until (and sometimes after) 6 P.M. for those last-minute customers who rushed in to get some paint for a child's school project that was due the next day. And he also understood why he couldn't hang up on a farmer who would call at 4 P.M. on a cold Sunday afternoon in winter, because he needed a part to fix a heater in his barn to keep his livestock from freezing that night. He would meet that grateful farmer at the store a few minutes later and open the store to get that part.

After I moved away from that town, and especially after my father died recently, I came to understand from his customers and neighbors just how highly he was respected and valued. He didn't see himself as a martyr, even though he probably would have liked to sleep a little later some mornings or take the occasional Saturday off, which he did all too rarely. He made his choices, however, and it was not until much later in life that he began to change them so they tilted toward his own needs just a bit more.

We each have choices to make—choices about how many of those 168 hours we want to spend working, thinking about work, or being on call in case someone needs us. I don't believe for a minute that most people are as choiceless as they think they are; the problem is that we often make the choices without realizing we've made them. We believe that we don't have a choice to make a choice, because we fear for our jobs or fear that we'll be seen as less than completely committed to our jobs, employers, and customers. And we don't realize that by choosing *not* to make a choice, we have in effect had a choice thrust upon us.

How the Three Time Zones Fit with Being "On Duty"

You have two specific decisions to make as you begin to change your approach to work and work time: how to divide up the week into three zones and how to define the extent to which you are willing to be "on duty" during each of them.

What follows is based on the assumption that your work is normally done primarily between Monday and Friday, and between what we have come to know as standard work hours of approximately 8 A.M. to 5 P.M. This doesn't imply that you should work only during those hours or on those days, but we'll use that traditional definition of the workweek—and the fact that there are only 168 hours in everyone's week—as the starting point.

Your first step is to decide how you want to define three different "on duty" levels; later, you'll allocate your 168-hour week (as well as vacation and holiday time) into these three levels. If we go back to the dry cleaner example, you'll remember that he was 100 percent "on duty" from Monday through Friday from 7 A.M. to 6 P.M. He was 0 percent "on duty" on Sunday (when he was closed), and he was, let's say, 60 percent "on duty" from 8 A.M. to 5 P.M. on Saturday.

The following weekly chart (Table 1) portrays his choices and decisions about how he spends his time. You'll note first in this key that the three "on duty" levels are shown with increasingly heavily shaded lines; this lets you view the weekly chart and quickly grasp the boundaries of those three time zones.

The weekly chart divides each day into one-hour blocks (reading across the top) and into seven days (reading down the left side).

You'll note in this chart that all 168 hours are accounted for, even though we've only spoken so far about the hours the store is open. By definition, the store is 0 percent "on duty" from 6 P.M. to 7 A.M. the following morning during the week, and on similar periods before and after the Saturday opening hours, and throughout Sunday.

You might be thinking that the store owner, like all small-business owners, probably does some of his paperwork in the evenings or even on Sunday, and therefore it's inaccurate to label those times as 0 percent. The reason I did so at this point is to emphasize that the definitions of "on duty" and "off duty" favor the effects on co-workers and customers/clients. Later, you'll see how to deal with the time you spend working after hours on work that isn't as directly related

Table 1

Time Block →	Mon.	Tues.	Wed.	Thurs.	Fri.	Sat.	Sun.
12 A.M.–1 A.M.							
1 A.M.–2 A.M.							
2 A.M.–3 A.M.							
3 A.M.–4 A.M.							
4 A.M.–5 A.M.							
5 A.M.–6 A.M.							
6 A.M.–7 A.M.							
7 A.M.–8 A.M.							
8 A.M.–9 A.M.							
9 A.M.–10 A.M.							
10 A.M.–11 A.M.							
11 A.M.–12 P.M.							
12 P.M.–1 P.M.							
1 P.M.–2 P.M.							
2 P.M.–3 P.M.							
3 P.M.–4 P.M.							
4 P.M.–5 P.M.							
5 P.M.–6 P.M.							
6 P.M.–7 P.M.							
7 P.M.–8 P.M.							
8 P.M.–9 P.M.							
9 P.M.–10 P.M.							
10 P.M.–11 P.M.							
11 P.M.–12 A.M.							

Key: Off Duty   Mid-Duty   On Duty

81

to others; for now let's assume that the dry cleaner's hours and on/off duty periods are based only on the customer-contact activities.

You should note these three points about this chart:

- Every hour of the 168 per week is accounted for and assigned to one of the three levels of being "on duty."
- The three levels of shading give you a quick visual tool to see approximately what portion is allocated to each of the three "on duty" levels.
- The 100 percent "on duty" periods designate the hours that the store is open and fully available for all services to customers. That doesn't necessarily mean that customers are actually in the store all of the time, though the owner might wish that was the case. This is an important distinction, because the key issue here is *being available and accessible* to others. Similarly, we'll see in the next chapter that you will define your time zones based primarily on whether you are expected to respond to phone calls, pages, and e-mail from others.

Why *60 Percent* "On Duty"? Why Not 40 Percent, or 75 Percent, or 90 Percent?

That's a good question. It's easy to understand what the 100 percent and 0 percent numbers mean, but that gray area of 60 percent (in the example above) is less clear. Be assured that there's nothing mathematically sacred about that 60 percent number; all I want is to label those hours during which you are neither fully "on duty" or fully "off duty." I've chosen 60 percent in this example to indicate (for the dry cleaner) that having the store open for customers to drop off and pick up their cleaning is something considerably less than if he were open for full service, yet it's still above the 50 percent level that would suggest to me that he's only providing half of his total services.

The good news is that you can pick whatever number makes sense to you: 30 percent, 80 percent, 67 percent, or anything else that tells *you* "This is the time when I'm less available and accessible than I would be during my 100 percent time." In fact, you can discard the percentage labels completely and replace them with an A/B/C or 1/2/3 or any other designation that feels right for you. This is nothing more than a simple, shorthand notation for how you think about your time in general. For the "mid-duty" period, the middle designation you choose says, "This is the time when I'm still working, but not as available, accessible, or responsive to others as I would normally be during the standard working hours."

This middle zone is vitally important because it's likely to be a new way of looking at your workload and your availability. We generally consider ourselves to be working or not working, but don't (consciously, at least) consider a defined middle ground between those two extremes. It is this middle zone—whether you choose to call it 60 percent, 80 percent, B, 2, or whatever suits you—that will help give you some breathing room in your busy week. You'll see how to integrate this "mid-duty" zone into your week's schedule in Chapter 5.

PUTTING THE "THREE ZONES" MODEL

TO WORK

Now that you understand the basics of the three zones, it's time to move from the conceptual to the practical and develop your own plan for dividing up the 168 hours that *you* are given each week. We'll start with a basic plan for a typical week and then you'll see how it can be modified to account for travel, holidays, vacations, and other departures from what's normal for you.

Creating Your Personal Time and Work Plan
Step 1: Define What "On Duty" Means for You

This might seem obvious, but it's worth taking a moment to confirm in your own mind what it means. "On duty" means that you are fully available, accessible, and willing and able to do your work. It doesn't mean that you are working every minute of every hour; it just means that this is the period during which you'll do most of your work and during which others who rely on you can reasonably expect to find you, reach you, or hear back from you in a short time if they leave you a message of any kind.

Time Out: Let's Consider Service Levels

That last paragraph is full of fuzzy language—terms like "most of your work" and "reasonably expect" and "in a short time." It's a good idea to pause here to clarify those terms in your own mind and for others—in effect, to do what's known as setting "service level agreements."

That term normally applies to activities such as response time from a help desk—"all messages received between 8 A.M. and 6 P.M. on Monday through Friday will be answered within 15 minutes." I'm not necessarily suggesting that you need that level of specificity in your own job, but ask yourself if you and your co-workers or customers would benefit from having it.

The advantages of clarifying those service levels are to:

• Greatly lessen the chance that what may be inherently different definitions of "soon" and "responsive" get in the way of smooth working relationships. Let's say that you and I work together and I normally check my e-mail every 30 minutes and you check yours every two hours. We both feel that our own chosen mail-checking interval is right, but it's likely that we will clash at some point because I think you don't check yours often enough and you think I'm obsessive about how frequently I check mine. This wasn't a problem in the days when most office work was done in the office and when most communication between co-workers was face-to-face or in real-time phone calls. It becomes a big problem today with so much reliance on electronic messaging of various kinds.

- Establish a benchmark for the expectations and response times you will establish during your "off duty" and "mid-duty" time zones. You've already seen that the basis of the three-zones model we're using is to define time periods when you will be *less* responsive and *less* available than you are during the normal work hours and days. It's much easier and more sensible to do that if you can define *how much* less responsive and available you'll be when compared to specifics in your "on duty" time zone.

It is very important to remember that you're setting these parameters not only for yourself (so you can create some breathing room in your own life) but also to clarify for others just how responsive and available you will be during certain times of the week. To say that you'll check your e-mail "often" or "frequently" during normal work hours during the week, and then to say that you'll check e-mail "*less* often" and "*less* frequently" during the evening or on weekends is not enough. Those fuzzy terms leave you wide open for the problems caused when others define these terms using their own expectations and not yours.

Back to Your "On Duty" Time Zone Definitions

Take a few minutes now to write down your own service level commitments for your "on duty" time zone. Keep in mind that these are your goals for what you'll do if nothing else more urgent gets in the way. For example, you might say that you'll check your e-mail once an hour; but if you're in a two-hour meeting you're not going to leave halfway through just because you have committed to yourself and others that you'll check e-mail every hour:

Check e-mail every _____ (circle one: minutes/ hours)

Check voice mail every _____ (circle one: minutes/ hours)

Respond to pages within _____ (minutes)

Work at the computer* continuously no longer than

_____

(circle one: minutes/hours)

---

* To this point the emphasis has been on work activities that relate to your accessibility and availability. Some of you—perhaps at the prompting of co-workers or significant others—might want to add this fourth item to cover the time you spend doing whatever you do on your computer. Even if that work doesn't involve answering e-mail, it is still time that isn't being spent on other activities. Partly for reasons of setting boundaries, and partly to prevent the aches and pains that can come from extended periods of computer work, this fourth item merits your attention as much as the other three.

Technological Twists to Consider

While you're thinking about those time intervals and service levels, a few words of explanation about today's technologies are in order.

Some corporate e-mail systems put a message on the screen or cause an audible signal when someone has sent you e-mail. You generally aren't obligated or forced to read the e-mail at that moment, but at least you have the notification. The fact that someone has sent mail (and thus triggered the on-screen message or tone) doesn't necessarily mean you have to interrupt what you're doing to read it, though you certainly can. The idea of setting an interval for checking e-mail refers to how often you will *stop* what you're doing and read any accumulated incoming messages, rather than how often you'll let yourself be interrupted to respond to those "screen pops" or tones.

This is another area to address when setting service level agreements. The good news about corporate systems that immediately notify people when someone has sent them e-mail is that the incoming message is like a postman who knocks on your door when leaving mail in your mailbox, instead of just leaving it without you knowing it's there to be retrieved. The bad news about these systems is that the instant notification can interrupt whatever else you were doing—and unless you're careful you spend the whole day being interruption-driven rather than work-driven. Some departments or teams of employees agree among themselves to respond to these notifications at once, but I think this can be a bad practice because the growing volume of e-mail means nobody would get anything done *except* respond to those interruptions.

Some work groups deal with this paradox of instant communication versus constant interruption by agreeing among themselves to use the various communication tools they have in a hierarchy of urgency. This is especially important if the work group is dispersed within a building, let alone spread out across a city or region if the group involves sales reps, telecommuters, and other mobile workers. Such a hierarchy might look like this, ranging from highest to lowest urgency:

- Find you in person and stand in front of your desk.
- Call you on the phone.
- Page you.
- Leave a voice mail message.
- Leave an e-mail message.
- Fax you.

The dispersed or distributed work team won't always be able to use the first option, and might be able to use the second option only if the mobile workers have cell phones. That's why paging is still an important tool, though it is being replaced in some cases by newer cell phones with a two-way-radio feature allowing members of a work group to call a colleague (within a limited geographic area) as if they were talking on walkie-talkies.

Finally, some work groups create their own ways to refine this kind of urgency hierarchy even further. Let's say the group has agreed on the hierarchy listed above and has further agreed that when one member pages another, the normal response time should be within 30 minutes. But if they're using numeric paging only, and the phone number that appears on the screen is followed by the numbers 911 (the standard North American telephone number to call in emergencies), that means the person sending the page has an especially urgent need and the recipient should respond as quickly as possible. The spread of alphanumeric paging makes the use of this 911 suffix (or other codes) unnecessary, but there are still lots of numeric-only pagers in use.

The purpose of taking a departure to explain these technology twists is to remind you that we're blessed (and sometimes cursed) with an increasingly varied and versatile set of tools. You'll be able to make better use of those tools, and get a better sense of how to make them work for you and not against you, if you understand what's feasible.

Creating Your Personal Time and Work Plan
Step 2: Define What "Off Duty" Means for You

Once you have spelled out what "on duty" means for you, the next (and easier) step is to pin down the opposite end of your work spectrum. If your "on duty" time is your 100 percent available and accessible time, your "off duty" time is when you are 0 percent available and accessible. In simple and stark terms, this is the time when you don't exist as far as your boss, co-workers, and customers are concerned.

You might be wondering just how impermeable that barrier is between you and your work during your "off duty" time. My advice, and what I have determined in my own situation, is that "off duty" *means* "off duty." It's not "I'm probably not working but if you *really* need something you can call me," or "I don't expect to be checking voice mail or e-mail but if I have a moment I might do so." As soon as you start hedging and let it be known that "you're not working unless it's really important," chances are that your customers or co-workers will leap into that crack you have provided in the armor around your free time.

It's impossible for me to know exactly what your job situation is and just how urgent things can be. If you're thinking that it's unrealistic to define "off duty" with such conviction and absoluteness, then you can decide where and how to create one or more of those little openings in the boundary. For example, it's likely that your boss has your home phone number and would use it to call you on a Sunday afternoon if it were truly a matter of utmost importance or consequence to your organization—and in that case, perhaps you wouldn't mind.

My only comment is that little cracks in the boundary around your "off duty" time can erode into larger openings, little by little and without any malicious intent on anyone's part. If you are willing to be vigilant and assertive in case those super-urgent situations begin to happen more often, then by all means you can and should make yourself accessible on that limited basis.

It's also important for you to carefully consider the benefit of keeping that boundary completely closed, or as close to completely closed as possible. For me, the time I'm "off duty" puts me in a different frame of mind because I have freed myself from even the possibility that I'll have to think about work.

How long has it been for you since you have:

- Turned off and taken off your pager;
- Turned off and not carried your cell phone;
- Not felt an involuntary twinge as your home phone rings on the weekend, wondering if it's something about work;
- Not felt guilty if you didn't call in once or twice for voice messages or checked for e-mail messages on a weekend, let alone on a holiday or vacation?

If you're like most people, it has been far too long since you've enjoyed the sheer pleasure of being unhooked, unwired, and unavailable. You may be struggling with the worry, guilt, or doubts about just how feasible it is for you to create a 0 percent, "off duty" time zone other than from, say, 1 A.M.to 5 A.M. It's impossible to push those thoughts out of your mind completely, but I suggest that you weigh them against the more pleasant thoughts about the benefits of doing exactly that.

With those points in mind, fill in this chart for your 0 percent, "off duty" time:

Check e-mail every _____ (circle one: minutes/ hours)

Check voice mail every _____ (circle one: minutes/ hours)

Respond to pages within _____ (minutes)

Work at the computer continuously no longer than

_____

(circle one: minutes/hours)

"Wait a minute," you might be thinking as you just filled out that chart—or if you hesitated before doing so. "Why am I

specifying these time intervals if this 'off duty' time is supposed to be my no-work time?" That's a good question, and
that's why your chart for this 0 percent time block should
most likely look like this:

Check e-mail ~~every~~ _____ ~~(circle one: minutes/~~
~~hours)~~ **Not at all**
Check voice mail ~~every~~ _____ ~~(circle one: minutes/~~
~~hours)~~ **Not at all**
Respond to pages ~~within~~ _____ ~~(minutes)~~
Not at all
Work at the computer continuously ~~no longer~~
~~than~~ _____
~~(circle one: minutes/hours)~~ **Not at all**

Is it that simple? Can you really "turn it off" that completely?
Only you know for sure. If you can, you will have created a
time zone that is truly yours and yours alone, without the
expected or unexpected intrusions from or about work.
Tempting, isn't it?

It's more than tempting—it's possible, as long as you do it
the right way. In Chapter 6 we'll look at methods for implementing this three-zones model in a way that doesn't get you
fired or cause you to lose your best customers. For now, your
task is to decide if you feel entitled to designate at least some
of the time that you now spend working as non-work time
instead, and (shortly) to develop your weekly schedule along
those lines. I hope you're able to agree at this point that it is
possible to be a dedicated, hardworking, committed employee (or business owner) *and* still give yourself the gift of
free time other than while you're asleep.

Creating Your Personal Time and Work Plan
Step 3: Decide on a Middle Range

Now comes the (slightly) more challenging part: how to handle the gray area between the two extremes. Most find it difficult to live in those in-between areas in many aspects of our lives; we can agree with the adage about "all things in moderation" until it comes time to, say, eat one cookie, not three, or exercise to the point of being tired instead of completely fatigued.

Here's where the advantage of having spelled out your service levels for your "on duty" or 100 percent time and your "off duty" or 0 percent time becomes clear. With those as the end points, your 60 percent or "mid-duty" time zone will be the time when your responsiveness is somewhat less than when you're on 100 percent, but considerably more than when you're "off duty" and at 0 percent. For example, if you normally check your voice mail every hour during the workweek (100 percent time) but not at all on weekends (0 percent time), you might choose to check it every three hours during your 60 percent time.

Remember that as you define these service levels for your "mid-duty" or 60 percent time, you're doing so based on your own decision about how much less than 100 percent "on duty" you want to be. Based on your interest in work, your personal and family situation, and other factors, you might actually consider your "mid-duty" time zone to be more like 80 percent. If you normally check your voice mail every hour during the workweek (100 percent time) but not at all on weekends (0 percent time), you might choose to check it every 90 minutes during your "mid-duty" time *if* you think that's a period that warrants 80 percent commitment.

Using the Three-Zones Charts

You'll see a series of charts throughout the rest of this chapter, all of which follow the same design and use the same shading key as the chart you saw in Chapter 4. The only difference is that the charts in this chapter divide each day into two-hour time intervals, unlike the chart in Chapter 4 for the dry cleaner that used one-hour intervals. That was done because some of his store hours began and ended with odd-numbered hours. The two-hour intervals on the charts in this chapter are suitable for most people; you can always go back and divide some of them in half if needed.

The first group of charts show—in progressive fashion—how a typical workweek might look, accounting for the three time zones. Later in the chapter, you'll have an opportunity to fill out your own charts from scratch based on your decisions about time use.

I can't emphasize enough how useful it will be to fill out these charts, either by writing on the ones printed in the book, or by photocopying the charts if it's easier to work with them separately. Don't be concerned about the actual graphics, dimensions, or any other features of these charts; they are included to give you a working tool at this point as you define your own time zones. You can certainly sketch out (by hand or on your computer) a different chart if you prefer. In either case, it is *very* important that you go through the process of filling in the charts—without that step, you're not as likely to get full value from this planning process.

Now it's time to make two decisions:

- What *does* "mid-duty" time mean to you? Is it the 60 percent I've been using or is it something higher or lower? Write that number here: _____
- Based on that number, what will your accessibility and response times be? Write those numbers in this chart:

Check e-mail every _____ (circle one: minutes/ hours)

Check voice mail every _____ (circle one: minutes/ hours)

Respond to pages within _____ (minutes)

Work at the computer continuously no longer than

_____

(circle one: minutes/hours)

Putting It All Together

Congratulations! You have just completed almost all the work needed to start bringing your time back under your control. Let's see how this adds up: first, fill in the chart on page 98 based on the numbers you used when defining your "on duty," "off duty," and "mid-duty" time zones. Write in the intervals/ durations you noted earlier for the four activities (going down the far left column) for each of the three time zones—and don't forget to write in your own *percentage* definition of "mid-duty" in the space at the top of that column.

It may not seem like you've accomplished much, but you actually have. You've taken what has been to this point an unconscious or subconscious use of your time and made some *deliberate decisions* about how accessible, available, and involved you want to be during three portions of every week. The next and final step—and perhaps the most challenging—is to define the actual hours or days that make up *your* three time zones. You'll do this in several steps, so it will be easy to see how to account for the entire week.

A good way to begin is with the two ends of the spectrum—your 100 percent and 0 percent zones—because those are most familiar. Let's say you choose to designate 8 A.M. to 6 P.M. on Monday through Friday as your 100 percent, "on duty" time, and (for now) from 6 P.M. Saturday through 10 P.M. Sunday as your 0 percent, "off duty" time.

Table 2 on page 99 shows how that might look.

As you can see, you have accounted for 50 hours (8 A.M. to 6 P.M. on Monday through Friday, which is your 100 percent time) plus 28 hours (6 P.M. Saturday through 10 P.M. Sunday, your 0 percent time) for a total of 78 hours so far. That leaves 90 hours of your 168 hours in each week to deal with, so let's continue.

Nobody, we hope, would disagree that you need to and are entitled to sleep, and it's unlikely that you're expected to answer phone calls or pages during the middle of the night, so you can now block off your normal sleeping hours plus some buffer time on both sides of your pillow time.

If you designate 10 P.M. to 6 A.M. on Sunday night through Saturday night as 0 percent time (for sleeping), you've accounted for another 56 hours and you can see how this looks on Table 3.

Congratulations! Now you're down to 42 hours to deal with: the white blocks in the chart with no shading at all.

Refer to Table 4 to see how those 42 hours would look if we view them alone.

You can see that the hours of 6 A.M. to 8 A.M. Monday through Friday (10 hours) plus 6 P.M. to 10 P.M. Monday through Friday (20 hours) plus 6 A.M. to 6 P.M. Saturday (12 hours) add up to these remaining 42 hours. Note that these are "in-between times"; for example, from 6 A.M. until 8 A.M. on weekday mornings you're awake, getting ready to go to work, and commuting to work, and from 6 P.M. to 10 P.M. weekdays you're commuting back from work and spending your evening at home before going to sleep. The hours on Saturday are also designated here as "in-between times," and as yet, these 42 hours have still not been assigned to any of the three time zones.

These hours might be the toughest ones to deal with. Should you, for example, be expected to check your e-mail and voice mail messages while you're getting dressed in the morning at home and while you're at home in the evening before you go to sleep? If so, then those become 60 percent or

	On Duty (100%)	Mid-Duty (___%)	Off Duty (0%)
Check e-mail every:			
Check voice mail every:			
Respond to pages within:			
Work @ PC no more than:			

Table 2

Time Block →	12 A.M. – 2 A.M.	2 A.M. – 4 A.M.	4 A.M. – 6 A.M.	6 A.M. – 8 A.M.	8 A.M. – 10 A.M.	10 A.M. – 12 P.M.	12 P.M. – 2 P.M.	2 P.M. – 4 P.M.	4 P.M. – 6 P.M.	6 P.M. – 8 P.M.	8 P.M. – 10 P.M.	10 P.M. – 12 A.M.
Mon.												
Tues.												
Wed.												
Thurs.												
Fri.												
Sat.												
Sun.												

Key: Off Duty   On Duty

99

Table 3

Time Block →	12 A.M.–2 A.M.	2 A.M.–4 A.M.	4 A.M.–6 A.M.	6 A.M.–8 A.M.	8 A.M.–10 A.M.	10 A.M.–12 P.M.	12 P.M.–2 P.M.	2 P.M.–4 P.M.	4 P.M.–6 P.M.	6 P.M.–8 P.M.	8 P.M.–10 P.M.	10 P.M.–12 A.M.
Mon.												
Tues.												
Wed.												
Thurs.												
Fri.												
Sat.												
Sun.												

Key: Off Duty — Mid-Duty — On Duty

Table 4

Time Block →	12 A.M.–2 A.M.	2 A.M.–4 A.M.	4 A.M.–6 A.M.	6 A.M.–8 A.M.	8 A.M.–10 A.M.	10 A.M.–12 P.M.	12 P.M.–2 P.M.	2 P.M.–4 P.M.	4 P.M.–6 P.M.	6 P.M.–8 P.M.	8 P.M.–10 P.M.	10 P.M.–12 A.M.
Mon.												
Tues.												
Wed.												
Thurs.												
Fri.												
Sat.												
Sun.												

Key: Off Duty   Mid-Duty   On Duty

101

"mid-duty" time zones. But if you *don't* feel obligated or expected to be available and accessible during those times, they become 0 percent or "off-duty" time zones. This is your decision and your choice—but for now, let's make those before- and after-work periods 60 percent time.

That leaves 6 A.M. to 6 P.M. on Saturday as the only time not yet assigned in this example. Once again, what do you feel expected and obligated to do during this time—and, more important, do you want to change those obligations? One option is to assign some of those 12 hours as 60 percent or "mid-duty" time if you feel it's important to be somewhat accessible on Saturday. If so, perhaps you'll say 10 A.M. to 2 P.M. is 60 percent time and the remaining hours are 0 percent.

Refer to Table 5 to see how your chart would look with these assumptions in mind.

If we add up the total hours for each time zone across the week, you end up in this example with:

> 50 hours as 100 percent "on duty" time
> 84 hours as 0 percent "off duty" time
> 34 hours as 60 percent "mid-duty" time
> 168 hours total

So much for this hypothetical example. Now it's time for you to start with a blank chart and design your own workweek. This is where the math is over and the analysis and your personal decision making begin in earnest. Earlier in this chapter, you designated the response or service levels for your own 100 percent, 0 percent, and whatever percentage you designated your "mid-duty" time to be. Keeping those definitions of the three time zones in mind, fill in this seven-day

Table 5

Time Block →	12 A.M. – 2 A.M.	2 A.M. – 4 A.M.	4 A.M. – 6 A.M.	6 A.M. – 8 A.M.	8 A.M. – 10 A.M.	10 A.M. – 12 P.M.	12 P.M. – 2 P.M.	2 P.M. – 4 P.M.	4 P.M. – 6 P.M.	6 P.M. – 8 P.M.	8 P.M. – 10 P.M.	10 P.M. – 12 P.M.
Mon.												
Tues.												
Wed.												
Thurs.												
Fri.												
Sat.												
Sun.												

Key: Off Duty   Mid-Duty   On Duty

103

Table 6

Time Block ⟹	12 A.M. – 2 A.M.	2 A.M. – 4 A.M.	4 A.M. – 6 A.M.	6 A.M. – 8 A.M.	8 A.M. – 10 A.M.	10 A.M. – 12 P.M.	12 P.M. – 2 P.M.	2 P.M. – 4 P.M.	4 P.M. – 6 P.M.	6 P.M. – 8 P.M.	8 P.M. – 10 P.M.	10 P.M. – 12 A.M.
Mon.												
Tues.												
Wed.												
Thurs.												
Fri.												
Sat.												
Sun.												

Key: Off Duty Mid-Duty On Duty

104

chart (Table 6) by allocating all 168 hours to one of the three time zones. You might want to make a couple of photocopies of this chart so you can experiment with different time allocations before writing the final version here.

Determining if Your Numbers Are "Right"

Now that you've completed your own chart from scratch, you're probably wondering if you've done it correctly. Before you try to answer this question, consider these two points:

1. Real Life Doesn't Follow a Chart. The purpose of making up this chart with the three time zones is to help you become more *conscious* about the *choices* available to you— and to encourage you to make those choices. It's ludicrous to assume that anyone can actually follow this chart to the minute in any given week; there are travel schedules, workload fluctuations, meetings, household responsibilities, emergencies, and a host of other things that are guaranteed to interfere with your neatly crafted schedule.

However, that doesn't mean the schedule is worthless. All it means is that this allocation of time into three zones is the *goal* you're aiming for, and a *benchmark* against which to measure how you will actually spend time in a given week. If you don't have a goal or benchmark, you're likely to continue watching the hours and weeks fly by and be consumed with more work than you might like—and thus be back in the same situation that prompted you to read this book.

2. This is *Your* Chart. While you may decide later to review this chart with your manager, co-workers, or significant

others, it's possible that nobody else will ever see it. This chart is a visual reminder about what you need to do to begin creating some boundaries between your work and the rest of your life. It isn't meant to be a schedule you expect others to agree to or treat as sacrosanct. However, in Chapter 6 you'll learn how to use the information on this chart to approach others and gain their support.

Having made those points, *are* these numbers right? *Do* you have too much "on duty" 100 percent time? At the risk of answering a question with a question, here's how you can do a reality check on your time chart. Ask yourself:

- Do the Time Allocations *Feel* Right? Based on instinct and intuition, do those numbers make sense to you? Can you live with those time distributions? These are difficult questions because you probably have never attempted to categorize your use of time this way, so you have nothing to compare that chart to except your own immediate, gut-level reaction—which counts for a lot.
- Have You Included Enough "Mid-Duty" Time? As was noted before, your "mid-duty" time is a new concept because you probably haven't previously set off a part of the week for time that you are working, but not *really* working. This kind of transition time is meant to let you maintain some responsibility to your work without being as fully involved with it as you are during your 100 percent time. As such, it's very valuable time because it's the period when you can begin to bridge between your work and personal lives.

- Have You Included Enough "Off Duty" Time? This is a good time to remind yourself that you *are* entitled to some no-work time other than when you're asleep. The days of the 40-hour workweek are gone, but they don't necessarily have to be replaced with the days of the 80-hour week. Use your "mid-duty" time to replace some of your 100 percent "on duty" time, and then be sure you have added in enough time when you're working at 0 percent—in other words, relaxing, spending time with family and friends, and taking care of personal business.
- How Do These Allocations Compare with What You Do Now? When you created your own three-zones plan, you did so based on what you believed was *ideal* for you, but not in comparison with your existing allocation of time. That's because you probably didn't use this kind of three-zones approach in the past, so there was nothing on which to base such a comparison.

Use the blank chart on page 108 (Table 7) for a full week to shade in your actual time allocations for last week or for a typical week. It isn't important to remember the exact hours you worked, slept, or did other activities. Just focus on your general use of time up to this point and divide it into the three zones; you'll have enough to make a comparison.

When you compare this chart with the one you created earlier, what kinds of changes do you notice? It's likely that you'll have more "mid-duty" time (which was taken from what had been 100 percent "on duty" time) on the new chart, and you might also have more "off duty" time. Are these changes satisfactory to you?

Table 7

Time Block ⟹	12 A.M. – 2 A.M.	2 A.M. – 4 A.M.	4 A.M. – 6 A.M.	6 A.M. – 8 A.M.	8 A.M. – 10 A.M.	10 A.M. – 12 P.M.	12 P.M. – 2 P.M.	2 P.M. – 4 P.M.	4 P.M. – 6 P.M.	6 P.M. – 8 P.M.	8 P.M. – 10 P.M.	10 P.M. – 12 A.M.
Mon.												
Tues.												
Wed.												
Thurs.												
Fri.												
Sat.												
Sun.												

Key: Off Duty   Mid-Duty   On Duty

108

- Would You Be Comfortable Telling Others About Your Allocations? It might be interesting for you to review your old and new charts with people who know your work and workstyle—co-workers, your manager, or your significant others. If you're uncomfortable actually doing that, you can imagine having a conversation with them in which you show them both charts and explain the differences. Whether real or imagined, those conversations will be helpful because you'll get (or pretend to get) feedback and comments that will validate the choices you've made, or perhaps challenge you to make further modifications.

- Do These Allocations Address Your Perceived Discomfort? You have read this far in the book and done the work because you are uncomfortable with how you are spending your time. How well do the new allocations deal with the things that you're dissatisfied with—and in particular, your "Techno-Mobile Resentment" scale answers from Chapter 2?

- Do These Allocations Seem Attainable, Even if They're a Stretch? Finally, you should review the new allocations to be sure they are within reach. If there isn't enough difference between how you're spending your time now and how you'd like to change, there won't be enough difference to motivate you to make a change. And if there's too much difference, it might be demotivating to even try to close the gap. You can always go through this charting exercise a few weeks or months from now and do some fine-tuning; in the meantime, make sure you're challenging yourself to change without setting yourself up for disappointment or failure.

How to Deal with Vacations and Holidays

You might have been thinking as you went through the chart making that nothing was mentioned about vacations and holidays. In fact, the only times that seem to have been designated as totally work-free in the examples were your sleeping hours and a portion of the weekend. We haven't ignored vacation and holiday time—we just left the best (but perhaps the most difficult) for last.

The premise of the three-zones model is that your analysis of and decisions about your time use and various levels of being "on duty" or "off duty" must begin with the standard, typical workweek. Vacations and holidays are important, but there are fewer weeks including them than weeks that are typical workweeks. Depending on where you work and your length of service, you probably have between two and six weeks of paid vacation each year, plus some number of one- or two-day paid holidays (e.g., Christmas, New Year's, and various local or national, or religious, holidays). Even a person who has as many as 8 weeks' worth of combined vacation and holiday time still has 44 workweeks each year, and those have to be considered first.

These three questions face you about your vacation and holiday time:

- To what extent are you *required* to be available and accessible during those times? The term "required" here connotes that as a condition of employment you *must* be reachable and *must* stay in periodic contact with the office—perhaps because of the critical nature of your job and/or the consequences to the organization if you aren't

110

available. The more you are required to be available and accessible, the more likely it is that at least some of your vacation and holiday time will fall into the "mid-duty" category.

- To what extent do you feel *obligated or expected* to be available and accessible during those times? The terms "obligated or expected" here imply that someone (usually your manager or a key customer) has told you or strongly hinted that you should be reachable and should stay in periodic contact with the office. In some cases, there might not have been any explicit request or even suggestion to stay in touch; you just may have picked up some subtle cues and clues that "that's how things are done around here."

- To what extent do you *want* to be totally unavailable and inaccessible during those times? This question speaks to your own needs and preferences. There are many people who don't necessarily feel they have to be completely disengaged from work while on vacation or holiday time, and there are others for whom the words "vacation" or "holiday" imply a total withdrawal from all things work-related.

The issue of accessibility and availability during vacation and holiday times is probably the most noticeable indication of the role of technology. It wasn't that many years ago that we didn't even have the option of being easily in contact with the office while on vacation or holiday unless we took the deliberate step to phone in and speak with whoever was keeping track of phone messages. That, plus the delivery of mail or packages by courier or overnight express services and perhaps occasional access to a fax machine at a hotel, was all we had at our disposal.

Cell phones, pagers, laptops, and near-ubiquitous access to a telephone jack today all mean it's much easier for us to be in contact and for others to find us when we're on what recently was always a retreat from work. This is the best example of the "just because we can doesn't mean we should" aspect of mobile-office technology. Just because we *can* check e-mail with a laptop from a seaside cottage doesn't mean we *should;* just because our boss or customers *can* call us via cell phone when we're out hiking in the mountains with the family doesn't mean they *should.*

It is interesting to see how the vendors are focusing on the technology versus vacation issue. An ad for Microsoft Windows2000 Professional began with this question: "Now you have the technology to work during your vacation. Does that mean you'll be doing more work, or taking more vacation?" The ad says that the software offers a great deal of "built-in mobility that lets you work wherever you want," to help cope with the blurred boundaries between work and free time. These mobility features let the user take the office on the road, says Microsoft. The last line of the ad asks, "Does the future of business mean work will become more like vacation, or vice versa?"

This strikes me as the fundamental question we all must answer as we sort through our technology options. Because vacations and holidays vary so much in duration, time of year, and proximity to the office, it's hard to come up with the same kind of charted time zones as you have done for the standard workweek. However, you can certainly do the following:

- Ask yourself what you *really* want to do about being accessible and available during vacations and holidays. Let's say you want to designate some or all of those times as 0 percent, "off duty" time but currently are required or feel obligated to do otherwise. If so, one of your main action steps to consider in this chapter is how to wean yourself and others off this kind of connectedness, and how to establish a more distinct boundary between the standard workweek and your holiday and vacation time.

- Ask yourself what the *real* consequences might be if you decide to make holidays and vacations part of your 0 percent time. Sometimes, organizational norms that develop about what you *should* do have little or no basis in the facts about what *will* happen if you *don't* do it. I'm not suggesting that you put your job on the line by arbitrarily deciding to take a stand and lead a one-person crusade against e-mail, voice mail, and phone calls during holidays and vacations. You might plan later to approach your boss, in a much more positive way, about getting disconnected while on vacation or holiday, but you can't even begin to do that without making a realistic assessment about the pros and cons of doing so.

- Consider whether you can create a slightly different kind of "mid-duty" time to cover vacations and holidays. Earlier in this chapter you defined your own 60 percent (or whatever number you chose) time based on your expected frequency of checking voice mail and e-mail and your timeliness in returning pages. Perhaps you might now create a 20 percent (or whatever number you choose) zone during which you would be less responsive and accessible than during your "mid-duty" time but more available than when you're in your 0 percent, "off duty" time. This new time zone might be a good compromise between going totally "off duty" (which is what you might want to do) and remaining at least at the "mid-duty" level (which is what your boss or customers might want you to do).

Vacation and holiday times are different from the rest of the work year. They exist for a purpose: to give you time off from the routine demands of the job. The more you allow or are required to let those routine demands seep into what otherwise is time off, the less valuable—to you and your employer and customers—those "vacations" and "holidays" really are.

It's *Your* Work-Life Balance That Counts

I have tried to avoid preaching or prescribing my own, or anyone else's, definition of how much time you should devote to work versus the rest of your life. The concept of work-life balance, as popular and important as it is, can be very elusive. While we may be sorely tempted to look at the person who works 80 hours a week and say that he or she doesn't have a good balance between work and personal time, it's dangerous to make those assumptions from afar.

There are many ways to achieve work-life balance. It doesn't always happen every week, simply by adding up the number of work hours and the number of non-work hours and categorizing that ratio as good or bad. That's an overly simplistic view and a potentially presumptuous one in which we impose our own definitions and needs on someone else. Balance can exist over a much longer time frame—for example, a series of those 80-hour weeks might be followed by a week or two with half as many work hours and/or a few "compensatory time" days off. That kind of occasional "time out" is enough to allow many people to feel that they're keeping all aspects of their life in balance—especially if, as many people do, they truly enjoy or believe in what they're doing and/or are willing to put in long hours for short periods.

Also, there's a new perspective developing on work-life balance that is perhaps more workable and sensible for many people. "Balance" implies a weighing and comparison of two separate, and often opposing, uses of time. Some believe that a more realistic approach is to think in terms of "work-life integration"—focusing on how well those two spheres of activity can mesh together instead of thinking about how they can be kept apart.

The Life of a 24-Hour Parent / Professional

Connie Goebel is a former client who describes herself as a recently released corporate warrior with more than twenty years of telecommunications marketing and sales experience, "including almost ten years of telecommuting under my belt." She now works as an executive recruiter with a search firm, but only goes into the firm's office one day a week. The rest of the time she works in her fully equipped home office with a powerful computer, cable modem, fax machine, two phone lines, cell phone, voice mail—the works.

We were talking about this book, and Connie got excited as

she realized how the boundaries between her work and personal time have become very permeable, to say the least. Her weekly routine provides a good example of how a seemingly hectic and interruption-driven schedule can actually be highly effective and satisfying. Here's how she describes how she manages to integrate her work with the rest of her life:

> Technology has enabled me to free myself from the traditional constraints of the office. I have voice mail on both my office and cell phone lines; this keeps me in touch with callers and lets me talk when I want to. My cordless office phone lets me roam around my home office—and my home—while waiting for an expected call or just being available for the unexpected ones. The cell phone gives me the freedom to call people from anywhere—even the gym.
>
> E-mail and the Internet give me access to messages and information 24 hours a day, if I want it. I don't have a laptop now—but hope to have one again soon, after having relied on one in my corporate jobs for the past eight years.
>
> My family, personal and professional activities are all important to me. When all are given a share (not always the same share or a fair share, but a share), I feel more balanced and at peace. So does everyone else.
>
> I try to do things when I feel I am at my best to do that activity. For example, I usually wake up early and my mind is racing. I get up, go into my home office and send e-mail long before the rest of the house knows it is morning. That gets me a head start

on my day, and gives me freedom to be with everyone else as they start theirs.

Most days I see my husband Jay and children (Alec, age 12, and Sally, age 9) at the beginning and end of the day. I can leave my office (sometimes with the cordless phone in hand) and brush hair, help with homework, listen to tales of woe, or even play a little basketball with them. When the weather is pleasant, after-school bike rides become a regular event.

This year I was able to be a room parent for Sally's classroom. She had been bugging me for years to do so; I never did it before for either child because I didn't have the flexibility or time to be able to commit to this responsibility.

Recently, I finally joined a gym—for the first time since before having the kids. Now I can go at off-hours, and take my in-box (trade journals, training manuals, etc.) to read on the exercise bike. I usually read a novel; however, I have read an average of three books a month since joining the gym. Reading is important to me—I have read a great deal since working more flexibly.

I'm able to get more involved in church committees because I don't travel as much for work and I make time to do church work at odd points in the day. It is no longer a situation where committee time has to be carved out of the scarce resource of family time. We have more family time now so other things can occur with less friction.

Basically, I work a nine to five schedule with time out for activities, doctor appointments, etc. as needed.

On the days I need to flex more than my workload
allows I try to find time to work early mornings,
evenings, and some on weekends (e-mail, calling,
leaving messages) to catch up. The key is that the
infrastructure is available so I can do the work if need
be at odd hours—but I don't work 24 hours a day. But
if I remember something I needed to do and want to
send a quick e-mail, I can do it while it's on my mind.

Having a separate office at home is very important. I have access to my work 24 hours a day, but
can close it off when I want to—though it can be difficult to do at times. My goal is to focus on the "now"
of where and who I am at any point in time.

Connie has figured out how to balance work and personal
duties, and in fact her schedule shows that she not only
balances them but also *integrates* them quite well. But I won-
dered about what seems to be missing from this schedule—
totally free time for herself and/or family, in which she is completely unplugged and disconnected from work. Does she
have that luxury, and if not, does she miss it?

I'd have to say that this whole schedule feels better
to me than any schedule I ever had. Not only do I
have free time, but for the most part I have control
over the "when and how much" of my work time.

Don't get me wrong—like most people I find there
is always more to do than there are hours in a day,
week, or month. But I have tried to divide up my life
into its most important parts and try to make sure
that I give something to each part each day.

Because "off duty" time is critical to me, I try to incorporate it into my schedule. It comes in several flavors: my "alone time" (to go to the gym, or for a walk or bike ride or to sit and read), and my time to be with family or friends. I guard those times jealously and try to plan around them—setting expectations with clients, applicants, and colleagues.

For example, we took several long-weekend ski trips this past winter. We leave home around 3 P.M. Friday to pick up the children at their respective schools. I usually have a few calls to make from the car, but that's better than staying in my home office to make the calls and then leaving later. But once the calls are done, the "office door" in my mind is closed until we return home. Similarly, I try to limit weekend or evening time in the office, and if something has to be done on the weekend I do it early Saturday morning so it doesn't interfere with my real life. Once I say I'm done working for the day or the week, I rarely check voice mail or e-mail until I'm ready to begin again.

Connie's schedule leaves me a little breathless—but it gives her just what she needs and lets her satisfy her manager, her clients, her family, and herself. That's what counts.

Some Last Thoughts on Planning Your Time—and Your Life

The process of setting up your three-zones chart, and especially of accepting the definition and role of the "mid-duty" time, can be a very effective way for most people to understand and act on their use of time. Depending on what's going on in your life, what your family situation is, how much you enjoy your work and have at stake with it, and what your short- and long-term goals are, you may decide to keep the number and distribution of your 100 percent, "on duty" hours exactly as they are—or perhaps even increase them. Or you might choose to ignore the idea of "mid-duty" time entirely because you'd rather be completely "on duty" or "off duty" if that's your best way to keep *your* work and life in the proper perspective.

Keep in mind that the purpose of this book is to help you make some informed, thoughtful decisions about what changes *you* need to make so you feel better about your work and your life, and the time you devote to each. Don't be swayed by the view that today's dedicated worker should be willing to do "whatever it takes, for as long as it takes" to do what's expected—a view that is especially pervasive in smaller and start-up organizations. Similarly, don't be influenced by the view that you're entitled to and should be able to enjoy a work schedule that lets you enjoy plenty of free time during which you're off the electronic tether and able to do nothing but rest, relax, volunteer, be with the family, pursue your hobbies or favorite sports and exercise, and so on.

My personal belief, as should be clear by now, is that our long-term effectiveness as employees or entrepreneurs is at risk if we spend week after week working at a fast pace and with little time to disengage and turn off our computers, cell phones, and brains. I hope by this point I've made the case that doing so can pay off for both employer and employee and have showed how you can understand your own needs and situation so you can plan to adjust your schedule accordingly.

I am not saying it's a sign of personal weakness or dysfunction if you choose not to make these changes. I may not agree, but neither I nor anyone else can tell you what you should do. Don't let yourself fall into the trap of trying to live your life according to what friends, family, co-workers—or consultant/authors—say about what might be best.

The reason I wrote this book is to help people look in the mirror and *examine* their use of time for work and personal activities, *decide if* they want to change, *create a plan* for changing, and *implement* that plan in a way that doesn't jeopardize their relationships with and value to their co-workers, manager, and customers. That's the process I went through myself and continue trying to fine-tune—but what's right for me is by no means right for you or anyone else. If you were to ask my wife or children, they might tell you that I *still* work too much and don't give myself enough of a breather. They're entitled to that view, but I'm more entitled to *my* view that what I'm doing is right for me and for them because I can find ways to fulfill my obligations to my clients, myself, and my family without any serious consequences for any of them.

The time you spend going through this process is just as valuable if you decide *not* to change anything or to make only some very minor adjustments. You will have come to that conclusion after a deliberate analysis of your situation, and your decision will be an informed decision and not an emotional or reactive one. If you do decide to make some changes, and especially if those changes are likely to affect your work relationships with your manager, customers, and co-workers, you'll find the next chapter especially useful because you'll learn how to implement those changes without risking your paycheck and career progress.

CHAPTER 6

How to Approach, Inform, and Get Support from Your Boss, Clients, or Co-Workers

I f you ended Chapter 5 with some excitement about how you can rearrange your work schedule to make it better meet your needs, you're ready for the next and most important step: getting the *support and commitment* you need from those who rely on your work.

"You Want the *Whole* Weekend Off?"

At this point most people experience a kind of approach-avoidance dilemma about putting their three-zones plan into action. They're anxious to get started because they feel confident and excited about how their lives might change if they use those three zones more effectively. On the other hand, they're hesitant—and sometimes downright scared—about

Facing the Boss

What will it be like for you to speak with your manager—or with your key clients—to discuss your interest in drawing some new boundaries between work and the rest of your life? Answer these four questions below to get an idea:

1. How would you rate the overall relationship between the two of you?
   a. Very Good—couldn't be any better
   b. Pretty Good—we get along well most of the time
   c. So-So—I never know what to expect
   d. Pretty Poor—most of the time we're at odds with each other
   e. Terrible—couldn't be any worse
2. How well do you keep your boss informed about progress and problems in your work?
   a. Very Well—the boss rarely gets any surprises
   b. Pretty Well—the boss knows about most of the important things
   c. So-So—sometimes I tend to withhold information
   d. Pretty Poorly—I don't provide much information at all
   e. Very Poorly—I don't divulge anything unless it's a disaster
3. How would your boss rate your dependability and reliability?
   a. Very Good—I meet all my deadlines and deliver what's expected

b. Pretty Good—I'm generally on time and deliver most of what's expected

c. So-So—I'm as likely to miss a deadline or a deliverable as not

d. Pretty Poor—most of my deadlines and deliverables are missed

e. Terrible—if I were the boss I'd probably fire me

4. How reasonable has your boss been when you've tried to negotiate something?

a. Very Reasonable—we can almost always find an agreeable solution

b. Pretty Reasonable—more often than not we can find a way to compromise

c. So-So—sometimes we compromise and sometimes not

d. Pretty Unreasonable—it's rare that we can jointly negotiate and find a way to compromise

e. Very Unreasonable—I can barely remember the last time my boss gave an inch

WHAT YOUR ANSWERS MEAN

- If you have at least three of four answers that are either a or b, you shouldn't have much problem at all, assuming you bring a well-conceived plan to the boss.

- If you have two or fewer of four answers that are either a or b, you need to plan your approach very carefully, because history suggests the two of you don't always see eye to eye.

> • If you have two or more answers that are either d
> or e you might want to think twice about bringing
> up the "turn it off" topic at all at this time; you
> might be better off trying to improve your overall
> relationship first.

talking with the boss or some key co-workers or customers about the fact that voice mail, e-mail, and pages might not be answered quite as quickly, and perhaps not at all, at times when they have come to expect responsiveness.

The prospect of walking into your boss's office and announcing that you'll no longer be spending your spare time on Saturday afternoons checking for and answering his or her e-mail might be as appealing to you as a double root canal at the dentist. If you find yourself facing this dilemma—wanting to make some changes but apprehensive about doing so— here are some points to keep in mind:

- You Won't Be "Announcing" Anything. When you approach your boss, or anyone else about the changes you want to make, you'll be going in with a plan and not a demand or one-sided announcement. This process isn't about career suicide; it's about maintaining and, if possible, improving the working relationships you already have.
- Focus on the Results. The process of working these things out with your boss is just that: it's a *process* that should bring you the results you seek. You might think you'll be uncomfortable initiating that process, but keep in mind that you're doing it to achieve some long-term results that should make a big difference in your quality of life.

• Consider the Alternative. If you're apprehensive about trying to make these changes, just think about what's likely to happen if you don't. Taking this first step is the key to creating some more separation between work and the rest of your life. If you don't get started now, you're not likely to create any lasting changes in the way you feel about your work in the context of your life.

• You're Not Going Alone. I won't be there with you, but I'll do the next best thing in this chapter: I'll give you plenty of tips and suggestions about how to smooth out your life without ruffling anyone's feathers. No guarantees, of course, but I'll prepare you for having some discussions that could dramatically change how you and your significant others feel about your work and your life.

Who Do You Need to Talk With?

The previous section addressed some of the concerns you might have about working with your boss about these time boundary issues, but as the chapter title notes, your co-workers and/or customers (internal or external) may also be involved. In fact, today's organizations are full of cross-functional teams, strategic alliances with other organizations, and other kinds of nonhierarchical relationships. The late-night e-mail you get is as likely as not to come from someone outside your "chain of command" and quite possibly from outside your organization entirely.

It's not hard to determine who might be affected by any changes you make in your availability—just think of the people from whom you received calls, voice mail, e-mail, or pages in the evening, on weekends, or on holidays or vacation within the last several months. You don't necessarily need to contact all of them; start with the ones who:

- Have contacted you more than once during the times that you're going to establish as your "mid-duty" or "off duty" times;
- Have been relentless or unrepentant about their intrusion into what most people would consider their personal time or free time;
- Are most likely to have their *own* work affected if they are not able to reach you during time off;
- Are most likely to complain to their boss or other powers that be if they are not able to reach you during time off.

These people, in addition to your boss and key customers, are the ones with whom you need to review your plans. Don't skip over the needs of your immediate co-workers; since members of a work group are often highly dependent on each other, your access and availability to each other must be taken into account. Much of what follows in this chapter is based on your interaction with your manager, on the assumption that he or she is the person whose support and cooperation you need the most. That doesn't mean you can ignore all those other people, however.

Face-to-Face Versus over the Phone

Conversations about something as important as the boundary between work and personal life should happen in person if at all possible. It's just too easy for the meaning to be lost if these occur on a phone call, let alone by e-mail or fax.

But with today's dispersed workforces and organizations, you might not have the luxury of actually sitting down for a personal discussion with key colleagues or customers, or perhaps even with your manager. If that's the case, weigh carefully the benefit of holding off on this discussion until you find yourself in the same place at the same time with that person—perhaps at an upcoming staff meeting, trade show, or other activity.

The adage about "striking while the iron is hot" applies here. You'll probably want to have this discussion while these issues are fresh in your mind and while your commitment to change is strongest. A delay of up to a few weeks might not be a problem, but anything longer than that probably means you need to have the exchange by phone or risk losing your momentum to change.

Everything that follows applies just as much to a phone call as to an in-person meeting. Obviously, you won't be able to judge body language and you may miss some of the subtleties of the conversation, but don't let that hold you back from acting *sooner* by phone rather than waiting *much later* to do it in person.

Consider Doing Some Advance Work

Whether you meet in person or over the phone, consider what you know about your colleague's preferred method of discussing important issues. Some people like the "read it first, then talk about it" approach; they need to see something spelled out on paper (or onscreen via e-mail) in advance so they can assimilate it and think about it before engaging in a real-time conversation. Others are "all ears"—they prefer to get right into the conversation and might want a written summary afterward. It's very important to profile the person you want to reach and adjust your method accordingly.

If you decide it would be advantageous to brief him or her in advance in writing, it's best to keep it at the general level—there's no need to get into the details of the three time zones and other specifics. Your goal is to clearly state the purpose of the upcoming meeting (whether in person or by phone); for example:

> Susan, thanks in advance for making the time (to meet with me/to speak with me on the phone) on (date and time). I know your schedule is full, but this is something that affects both of us.
>
> I've been giving a lot of thought to the issue of the amount of time I spend at work or working away from the office, and especially when work seems to run into the evening, weekends, or vacations. I think you know I enjoy my job and am willing to do what's needed to meet my commitments to this organization. However, I've also begun to think about what's needed to take care of my personal (and family) life outside of work.
>
> It seems this has become more of an issue as we've all gotten used to using laptops, cell phones, pagers, e-mail and voice mail, and all the other tools we take for granted. The good news is that we can be reachable just about anywhere and anytime, but this

also means it's hard to draw the line between work time and other time.

What I'd like to discuss with you is some thinking and planning I've been doing that will let me continue to do my job as well as I can, and will also let me reserve just a bit more time for myself. I'm finding that as the workday and workweek become longer and almost merge into nights and weekends, I'm not able to give myself the time I need to get "disconnected" from work so I can recharge for the next day or next week.

I'm thinking that having somewhat clearer boundaries between work and non-work time will help me do a better job for you in the long run. Rest assured that I'm not looking to cut back to a 40-hour week or anything close; those days are gone. And as you know, I'm certainly willing to pitch in when something urgent needs to be done.

My goal in our talk is to go over how we can both get what we're looking for, because I certainly want to keep on contributing as a member of this team. I'm looking forward to (meeting/speaking) with you; thanks in advance for your cooperation and time.

If you reacted to that by thinking, "I would *never* use those words!" that's fine. I wouldn't expect you to use those exact words; they're only an example. Use *your own* words and *your own* style to convey the same message: your appreciation for his or her willingness to meet, your statement of the situation, a general idea of your objective, and a confirmation of the importance and likely value of the meeting.

It makes no difference whether you do this in three sentences or thirty, by e-mail or by voice, or in a serious tone or a lighter tone; choose the style that fits *your* style. This discussion is too important to you to rely on a "seat of the pants" approach without any prior notice.

The Six Steps for Success

Here is a systematic approach for putting your plan into effect. As you'll see, this should be treated just the same as any project or important responsibility that would normally be part of your job. That's not a coincidence; you *should* be thinking of this as an important responsibility:

1. Plan—Don't Improvise. A sure-fire way to fail in your efforts to bring your time use back under control is to simply walk into your boss's office on the spur of the moment. Although the topic of how you use your time may not seem to be as important as last quarter's budget, that's no reason why you should take it any less seriously.

You don't need to write out a word-for-word script, but it helps to at least outline your points so you can refer to them as you talk—and perhaps you want to give a copy of your outline to your boss or whomever you're speaking with. Having that outline prepared conveys a sense of purpose and says that the topic is something to which you have given serious thought. That will help you get an equally serious response because it won't appear as if you're just acting emotionally.

2. Recommend—Don't Beg. Don't go into this meeting with an attitude that you're asking for permission to get

your life back. You're approaching this as a business solution to a business problem; the fact that it involves some personal issues makes it no less relevant to your overall performance. If you are perceived as whining, complaining, or asking for approval in the same way as a child might approach a parent, you might be treated like that child and not as an adult.

When you started working in your current position, you didn't sign away all 168 hours of the week in the name of the organization. You were hired because you and your employer believed you would work hard, deliver the expected results, and add value to the work of others. In exchange, you would be given certain compensation, benefits, "perks," chances for advancement, and other forms of reward and recognition.

The job represented a fair balance between what you would be asked to give (or give up) and what you expected in return. If you feel that balance has shifted in favor of the employer, and at personal cost to you, you're within your rights to propose a thoughtful, businesslike solution. Don't undermine your own case by acting as if you're on bended knee to ask for relief.

3. Propose—Don't Impose. Now that I may have inspired you to go in with your head high and your objectives clear in your mind, let me caution you not to go overboard. The purpose of the meeting is to state your view of the problem and your recommended solutions, not to unload six months' worth of frustration on your boss or whomever. The meeting is about jointly developing a solution, not about shoving your own decisions down someone else's throat.

There's a fine line between being assertive and being aggressive, and those terms are often used—incorrectly—interchangeably. Some of the synonyms for "assertive" are "assured," "confident," "energetic," and "positive"—while the alternatives for "aggressive" include "defiant," "dominant," "intensive," and "pushy." A friend of mine has a simpler way to differentiate between the two; he says that an aggressive statement is one that has the phrase "you dummy" implied at the end, by virtue of the words, tone, and mannerisms you use.

There's no reason not to share your sense of frustration about how work has spilled over excessively into your personal life and time; in fact, your pitch will be that much more powerful if you convey some examples. Just make sure you don't do so in a way that can be seen as a personal critique or attack on the boss. You want your views and proposals to be listened to and accepted, not immediately rejected simply because you put the boss or whomever on the defensive.

This is important for two reasons: first and most obvious, you're trying to gain some awareness of and acceptance for your proposals and the problems that stimulated them. Second, no matter what the outcome of this meeting, you still have to work with this person just as you have in the past. If you poison what had been a good (or at least tolerable) working relationship with angry and accusatory statements, it's going to be very hard to carry on after this meeting.

4. Find and Fix Causes—Don't Treat Symptoms. There are two reasons you're getting phone calls, voice mail, e-mail, or pages at times you'd rather not. One is that the other person has a genuine need for information, help, or something else you have or can do. The other is that the person is trying to reach you because he or she is reacting to an underlying problem that, if solved, might make it unnecessary for that

Ten Things Not to Say to the Boss

Here are some sure-fire conversation stoppers—avoid these and any phrases like them at all costs:

"You *ruined* my last two vacations and my family hates you."

"Don't you think I have a right to *any* personal time to myself?"

"Just because *you're* a workaholic, don't assume everyone is."

"I thought we're supposed to work a 40-hour week—what happened to *that* idea?"

"Just what was *so* important that you had to call me at 9 P.M. last Friday night?"

"If I spend any more time working, *you're* going to be responsible for my divorce!"

"I'm getting calluses on my fingers from answering all *your* worthless e-mail."

"Do you have *any* idea how much I'm beginning to hate the sight of my laptop?"

"Go ahead—*send* me your e-mail while I'm on vacation. But don't hold your breath waiting for a reply."

"*Nothing* we do around here is worth my being interrupted by a pager during my kid's soccer game!"

contact on a Sunday afternoon. Differentiate between the two and you're likely to be able to make life easier for everyone, not just yourself.

Consider this example: let's say a co-worker or key customer contacts you repeatedly to ask questions about inventory status or pricing. Every time you get one of these calls or e-mails, you can find the answer fairly quickly simply by logging on to the corporate network and checking the system that holds this information, which you then relay back to the other person. In this case, the symptom is the request for information, but the underlying problem may be that the other person doesn't know how to access this same information for him- or herself, or perhaps hasn't been given approval to do so.

It may seem hard to believe, but you can't assume that everyone knows what's on increasingly large and complex corporate networks any longer. The reason you're getting those weekend calls or e-mails may be nothing more than the fact that nobody taught that person where that information is and how to get at it.

If you can spend a few minutes showing or telling the person exactly how to log on to the specific system and how to find those inventory numbers or prices, you'll make things better for both of you. Depending on how complex that task is, you can also offer, for example, to e-mail him or her a note summarizing the steps you just described so that person will have a resource to which he or she can refer. Doing that makes it easier for others *and* greatly reduces the chance they'll call you again next time because they forgot what you just explained.

There are many other examples of this symptoms versus causes problem, such as:

SYMPTOM: The employee whose performance is somewhat marginal and who reaches out to you for help, information, or guidance instead of handling something alone.

TYPICAL RESPONSE: You have to take time out of your weekend or vacation to answer his or her questions or correct mistakes.

LASTING SOLUTION: Train that person, show him or her how to do things right the first time, and if all else fails, encourage a transfer to a more suitable position or consider firing him or her.

SYMPTOM: The production line that seems to create more than its share of calls for emergency repairs.

TYPICAL RESPONSE: You get paged in the middle of the night at least twice a week and have to orchestrate the requests for maintenance help.

LASTING SOLUTION: Bring in the engineers or designers to study the real causes of the problems and find a solution that fixes the design flaws that lead to all the breakdowns.

SYMPTOM: Your counterpart in Asia thinks nothing of calling you or paging you on the weekend to review the progress he or she has made in the prior week on an important project to which you are both assigned.

TYPICAL RESPONSE: You listen patiently as the person goes through a highly detailed review of tasks completed, because you don't want to appear uninterested or discourteous.

LASTING SOLUTION: Ask the person to e-mail you a weekly status report, which you promise to review and comment on within 48 hours, or schedule time

for a weekly conference call at the end or beginning
of each week while both of you are still in the office.
Even though this might mean you have to arrive
early or stay late that day (because of time zone differences), it's still better than having your weekend
interrupted.

Those examples aren't as much about controlling your
use of time as they are about standard problem-analysis and
solution processes. You're correct if you're thinking that
these kinds of problems should be addressed and solved—for
good—without having to drag them into the kind of meeting
we're discussing. But the fact is that we all tend to treat symptoms rather than problems; it's faster and easier in most
cases. The good news is that the process of understanding
why you're being interrupted or expected to handle those
calls and pages over the weekend, for example, will help
solve the problem at hand and help you establish more "mid-
duty" or, ideally, "off duty" time.

5. Recap—Don't Race Away. I've heard the following story
attributed to everyone from General George Patton to President Lyndon Johnson to the legendary New York Yankees
manager Casey Stengel: when asked what his secret was for
getting younger subordinates to develop and to accept his
guidance, George (or Lyndon, or Casey, or whoever) allegedly
said, "I tell them what I'm going to tell them, I tell them, then
I tell them what I told them."

That one sentence boils down decades and volumes of
management and leadership training into twenty powerful
words, and it's good advice to follow in this context, too.
We've already established the value of setting the stage for

the meeting—either in advance or at the outset of the meeting—by stating why you want to have this discussion; that's the "tell them what I'm going to tell them" part. The content of the meeting itself is, of course, the "tell them" (or more correctly here, the "tell them and discuss with them") part. The third and final step is the one most often overlooked, yet it may be the most valuable.

Before you walk away from the meeting, or hang up the telephone, take a few moments to summarize what the two of you have agreed on and what, if any, action steps might need to be taken.

6. Reinforce—Don't Ignore. The results of this entire process of involving others in your plan to change the way you allocate your time depend on how well they comply with your requests. You're trying to create a change in their behavior, and as with all kinds of behavior change, a little reinforcement goes a long way toward having that new behavior continue.

Don't think of "reinforcement" in terms of giving food pellets to rats in a laboratory maze, even if that's how your job makes you feel sometimes. The kind of encouragement and recognition I'm suggesting includes:

- Letting a co-worker (who normally would call you or e-mail you a couple of times each weekend but didn't this past weekend) know that you appreciate the change, with a quick Monday-morning comment such as "Thanks for holding off until this morning before calling me; I appreciate being able to get a break over the weekend";
- Leaving voice mail for your boss to acknowledge that you know he or she was working late on the budget last

night and didn't page you for help—and offering to meet later on in the morning in case you can help with the final revisions. This approach shows that you both recognize your boss's situation and are willing to assist if you can.

You don't have to become obsessed with reinforcing every little change that someone else makes, but you should certainly try to recognize the big changes made by the people who create the most intrusions into your personal time. If they feel you don't acknowledge their restraint, they're likely to go back to their old ways in a hurry.

Five More Tips for Productive Discussions

Those six steps form the foundation of your plan for meeting or talking with others whose work habits affect how well you can create a boundary between your work and your life. Here are some additional pointers about what you can do before and after those meetings:

1. Choose the Time and Place Carefully. This may sound trivial, but it's almost as important as the content of the meeting itself: you have to find a suitable time and setting for your discussions to help ensure they are given the attention they deserve. There are some times that are obviously bad—such as first thing on a Monday morning or at 4 P.M. on a Friday afternoon—but you should also try to avoid times when your counterpart won't be able to give the topic complete attention. If, for example, he or she is busy preparing for a big client presentation coming on Wednesday, schedule your

meeting on Thursday or later to avoid the stressful period before the presentation.

Where you should meet is based on what space is available and how private and quiet it can be. If you can meet in your office or the other person's, and can close the door, that's a plus; if you work in an open-plan office you'll be better off finding a small conference room, a quiet corner of the cafeteria when meals aren't being served, or perhaps a restaurant outside of the building. The value of finding a distinctive place for the meeting is to convey something about the special purpose and value (to you) of the meeting.

If the person you're speaking with is located a few time zones away and you'll have to meet over the phone, you obviously have fewer options for meeting settings. At the very least, make sure that your location is quiet and one in which you can give the topic full attention. This is definitely *not* the kind of meeting to have on your cell phone while you're fighting commuter traffic on your way home.

2. Put Yourself in Their Shoes. As was noted earlier, it's important for you to look beyond your own frustrations and needs when engaging someone in a discussion about work schedules and free time. It's painfully obvious to you how *you* feel about these issues; you also need to carefully consider how *they* will feel.

For example, if that person doesn't call you or isn't able to expect you to respond to e-mail over the weekend, how might that affect his or her work? Are you going to create some more "off duty" time for yourself at the expense of that person's own scheduling or job performance? If he or she now has to wait until Sunday evening or Monday morning before getting your e-mail response, will that interfere with his or her schedule? You're much more likely to gain that person's cooperation if you *show* you understand what he or she faces and are willing to compromise if at all possible so your desire for more "mid-duty" or "off duty" time doesn't stand in the way of what that person is expected to do.

3. Sell Benefits, Not (Only) Features. The process of talking with those whose support you need to implement your time plan has been described thus far as a "discussion," which it is. However, it's also a bit of a sales pitch since you're trying to convince someone to do something he or she might not otherwise do.

I distinctly remember one of my responsibilities in my early corporate years: teaching a sales training course for newly hired sales representatives. One of the key messages we tried to convey to those reps was the difference between features and benefits, and the overwhelming advantage of selling the latter.

That section of the sales training course included a role play in which the sales rep would try to sell a vacuum cleaner to a housewife. (I *told* you it was during my "early corporate years.") One of the features of the cleaner was its 20-foot-long power cord; that fact by itself didn't sell many cleaners until it was coupled with the benefit statement ". . . and that means you can vacuum your house faster because you won't have to stop as often to plug the cord into another outlet. In fact, our vacuum cleaner has the longest power cord of any vacuum on the market today!"

The length of the cord (the *feature*) was perhaps interesting to the customers but not convincing; the fact that the longer cord would help finish the job faster (the *benefit* provided by that feature) really got their attention and helped make lots of sales—at least during our training class. The same thing applies when you're trying to gain someone's commitment for your plan. The fact that you'll be checking your voice mail or e-mail less often on the weekend is the feature; the benefit to your "customer" is that you'll be better able to support them the following week because you will have had a chance to catch your breath.

Emphasizing benefits over features isn't the same as trying to trick someone into agreeing with you. It's a method that helps gain commitment because it answers that all-important question "What's in it for me?" In this case, the "me" is the other person, and you need to think carefully about what benefits your plan offers to that person. And if you can't think of any benefits that are credible and will have perceived value, then don't even try to creatively invent some.

4. Stress the Benefits, but Don't Evade the Possible Problems. If you're trying to act maturely and honestly with your counterpart, you certainly can and should emphasize the benefits but you have an equal responsibility to face up to the possible problems. If you don't—and there will *always* be problems—you risk being seen as deceptive and acting only on your self-interest.

For example, let's say you want to stop taking your laptop on vacation so you can check e-mail twice a day as you have been told, asked, or "encouraged" to do. The benefit to you of freeing yourself from that electronic leash while on vacation is pretty clear, but your request to do so will probably trigger an immediate response like, "That's impossible! What are we going to do if we have questions about the research projects you're working on? We can't afford to wait until you get back from your vacation."

What you must desperately *avoid* saying and doing at this point is to smile, wave your hand as if to dismiss that concern, and say something like, "Don't be silly. You're probably not going to need me for anything. And if you do, I'm sure someone else can fill in for me." Here are the three problems with that response and some suggestions about what else you could do and say:

- When you smile and "wave away" the problem, you imply that the person's concerns are not valid and in fact are frivolous—and by extension, you are seen as self-centered and unwilling to meet someone else's needs.
  INSTEAD: listen carefully to the person's concern, nod to convey that you are paying attention, and don't start speaking until you're sure he or she is done.

- When you say, "That's silly," you are explicitly minimizing that person's concerns and implying that he or she is "just kidding."
  INSTEAD: make sure your first response is to briefly restate the concern to ensure and confirm your understanding. Above all else, people with complaints or concerns want to know that they are being heard and that someone is paying attention to them and to what's on their mind.

- When you say, "You're probably not going to need me for anything. And if you do, I'm sure someone else can fill in for me," you are further minimizing that person's concerns. Also, you may be creating the feeling that you're going to leave that person high and dry and stuck with a problem when you suggest that a vague "someone else" can fill in for you.

INSTEAD: acknowledge that there may be times when that person will want to contact you, and in fact, you might mention one or two recent incidents to show that you're very much aware of the kind of situation the person has in mind. Next, provide specifics about who will cover for you while you're away, and what steps you have taken or will take to ensure that those backups will be ready and able to assist this person.

As you can see, a frank and honest exchange about the other person's concerns is much more likely to cement his or her support than if you try to ignore those concerns or change the topic to something else.

5. Be Proactive—Inform Others in Advance. You can have the most carefully crafted plan in the world and have solutions for all the potential problems, but there's one more item on your to-do list. You need to be sure to let others know in advance, and very specifically, how your new schedule will affect your availability.

This relates to the topic of service levels that was discussed in Chapter 5, and the expectations that others have for how and when they can get hold of you and hear back from you when they leave you a message. As difficult as it may seem to get others to buy in to your plans to be somewhat less accessible, it is infinitely easier than dealing with their frustration and anger that will result if you don't let them know. This is true for your time periods that will become "mid-duty" hours, but especially important for the "off duty" hours and days—including holidays and vacations, if you have designated them as such.

A sure-fire way to lose whatever support you had been able to gain from your boss through this process is to put him or her in the middle between you and your co-workers, other managers, or customers. If your manager hears from those other people that they didn't get a response in a way and during the time when they had every reason to expect a response, you're going to have a lot of explaining to do. Having your boss's agreement is necessary but not sufficient; you have to go the next step and *communicate* how your three-zones plan will affect everyone else around you.

Take Time Out to Prepare and Practice

At this point you should have a good understanding of why you're going to have this discussion with your boss, co-worker, customer, or others. You should also be confident that you know how the conversation will flow and how to structure it so it's most likely to be received positively and acted upon as you like. Before you schedule the meeting or phone call, consider having a practice session—call it a rehearsal—with a friend or colleague.

There are three reasons for doing this last bit of preparation:

- First Try = Best Try. Chances are you'll only get one opportunity to have this discussion and get what you want. If things don't go well the first time, you can certainly schedule a follow-up meeting—but if you do, remember that the other person will also have more time to think about what you're saying and to prepare his or her reasons why *not* to agree with your request. As the old saying goes, "You never get a second chance to make a first impression."

- Make It "Trial and Success." If you practice with a friend who knows (or knows about) the person with whom you'll have the discussion, that friend can role-play well enough to counter your presentation with some realistic objec-

---

Key Points to Remember About Approaching the Boss

1. Look in the Mirror. Before you go in to the boss, look at yourself in the mirror and ask, "Would *I* agree to what I'm proposing if *I* were the boss?" Be honest: if you know you have some weak points in your argument, take more time to get prepared beforehand.

2. Anticipate, Anticipate, Anticipate. It's not enough to think about what you're going to say—you have to think through how the boss is likely to respond, and how you'll handle those responses. Don't rely on your ability to improvise on the spot.

3. Bosses Aren't (Generally) Ogres. Sure, there are some bosses who seem to thrive on making life miserable for their employees, but they're the exception. If you can muster a reasonable argument and a detailed plan, go into your meeting with a positive attitude about your likely success.

---

tions. It's far better to hear, think about, and have a chance to come up with responses to those objections when you practice rather than in the real discussion. This kind of practice can turn the discussion from "trial and error" to "trial and *success*" especially since your friend can brainstorm possible responses and alternative approaches.

• Confidence Aids Competence. There probably isn't anyone who would actually look forward to having the kind of discussion we've been considering here. You're going to talk or meet with someone who relies on you and probably has some authority or control over you, and ask that person to agree with your plan to be less available and accessible—which at least initially might make things more difficult for him or her. That isn't the kind of discussion that anyone has had much training for, and if you're trying to be sure you handle it well you need to be confident in your own abilities. The more confidence you can muster (based on practice), the more competent you will feel and the more likely it is that you'll achieve the outcomes you seek.

How the Discussion Might Sound

To help you better understand what to expect in this kind of discussion, here's an abbreviated version of the dialogue that might occur between a time-starved employee and his or her boss. This is definitely *not* a script or a model—it's just a hypothetical, but realistic, example of what you might encounter. This example should help you to better visualize the flow of this kind of discussion and thus will help you become more prepared and confident.

First, Some Background

This conversation takes place between Lee Williams (LW) and Mary Benedict (MB). Lee is a product manager in a consumer packaged goods company and Mary is the director of product management. Lee was originally hired as a field sales rep, has been in this job for about two years, and by all accounts is doing well. Lee gets good reviews, enjoys the work, is well accepted by co-workers, and in the eyes of senior management is thought to have potential to move up.

However, Lee has become increasingly concerned about how the demands of the job are spilling over into personal and family time. It wasn't always this way, but in the last six months it seems that the workweek hardly ends. Weekend phone calls from Mary and others plus a feeling that e-mail and voice mail have to be checked at least every 30 minutes even well into the evening and on weekends are becoming problems that must be addressed. Lee spoke briefly, and only very generally, to Mary last week about these issues and asked if they could set aside an hour today—a Wednesday—for a meeting:

LW: Thanks for agreeing to see me, Mary. I know how busy your schedule is with these two product launches coming up.

MB: You said it. It seems we barely get a chance to breathe around here.

LW: Well, that's what I'd like to talk about. Mary, I think you know that I like my job and enjoy working on these new-product launches. Since I transferred in from the field sales force, I can't believe how much I've learned and done. But in a way, I'm starting to feel like the work is sort of non-stop, as you were saying a minute ago.

MB: That's for sure. Just last week I promised myself I'd try to take at least one full weekend day completely off from work, but that idea went out the window when I got the new launch schedule from Operations on Friday. We're really going to have to hustle.

LW: Yes, I saw that. Looks like they're going to get the first batch of new product ready to ship about a month earlier. That's great news, of course, but I don't know how we're going to get everything done.

MB: It's simple—we'll just have to put in some more hours and take a temporary leave of absence from our personal lives.

LW: That seems to be happening to all of us. In fact, the more I've been thinking about it, the more I'm a bit concerned about it.

MB: Oh—how so?

LW: Let me give you a couple of examples. In our house, we have a tradition where I read a story to the kids before they go to sleep; I've been doing that since they were very young. No matter how crazy the day has been, it's nice for us to have a little quiet time together. They like it and I like it. Two nights ago I realized—as I was working in the den and heard the kids getting into bed—that I had read to them only once or twice in the last two weeks. Normally, the only time I miss it is if I'm away on a business trip.

MB: I can see how that might upset you.

LW: Also, my basketball game seems to be going to pieces. . . .

MB: Your *basketball* game? Aren't we giving you enough work to keep you busy?

LW: Actually, that's sort of the problem. A bunch of us in my neighborhood have gotten together for a Saturday-morning game every week for close to a year. Believe me, we're *far* from professional material—but it's a great way to get some exercise. Anybody missing those games suffers severe teasing from the rest of the gang.

It dawned on me that I'd missed one and sometimes two games a month for the last few months because I've been home working. And last weekend when I *was* there for the game, someone said I was playing like my body was in the gym but my mind was somewhere else. That really made me think.

MB: Lee, I know these last few months have been tough on you. They've been tough on all of us. But that's how things are these days; we're all trying to do more in less time. There's nothing I can do about it.

LW: That's just it, Mary. I think there *is* something we can do about it, and I've been giving it a lot of thought. I'm not trying to duck out of my share of the work, but I've decided that I need to find a way to get a bit more of a break in some ways.

MB: *You've* decided? Well, that's interesting. What did you have in mind—walking out of here at 4:30 every day and spending your weekends at the lake?

LW: That *would* be nice, wouldn't it? But that's not realistic, and I think you know me well enough to know that I'm not looking for that kind of schedule. I'd simply like to try to create a little more separation between my work and the rest of my life. As it is now, I'm feeling like I don't get a chance to get a breather. If I'm not *at* work I'm *thinking* about work, or answering *e-mail* about work, or *talking* to one of the team about work, and so on. It didn't dawn on me how much this was happening until my neighbors on the basketball court mentioned it, and until my kids asked me, "How come you aren't reading to us?"

MB: Well, I can see how those things would make you stop and think. But as I said, I don't know how you can expect to cut down your workload; you know the pressure we're under to deliver first-rate product launches.

LW: I don't want to cut down my workload—I just want to try to *contain* it a bit more. I'm starting to think that my ability—in fact, *our* ability—to get those products launched correctly might suffer if we all don't get a chance to separate ourselves from work and get recharged a bit. Otherwise, it feels like we're on a treadmill that never stops. After a while it's hard to keep up that pace without stumbling.

MB: You won't get an argument from me on that.

LW: Here's what I've been thinking—it seems to me that I've sort of slipped into a mind-set where my work and work-week have crept into times and days that normally would be time off, or at least, time when I wouldn't have been expected to answer phone calls or return e-mail. I wouldn't trade my laptop, my pager, and my e-mail access for anything; what I want is to find a way to have them intrude a bit less into my life.

MB: So what do you suggest—turning off your pager after 6 P.M. and not checking e-mail on the weekend?

LW: Not exactly. But you're not far off. I'd like to come to an agreement with you about the times of day and the days of the week when it's okay to be a little less available and accessible to you and the rest of the department. Frankly, I'm starting to feel like my laptop, pager, and voice mail are tools that are dragging me down and tying me up instead of helping me.

MB: I'm starting to get the picture, but I still don't see exactly how you expect things to change.

LW: Let's take e-mail and voice mail, for example. We've all pretty much agreed that we're going to check both at least once an hour during the workday, and if someone needs an immediate response we can be paged and have to respond within 15 minutes. Those are reasonable expectations, but I'm having trouble with the fact that they seem to extend into the evening and weekend hours as well.

   I'm thinking that if I can just make myself less obligated to check e-mail and voice mail quite as often, and also designate some times when I'm not going to check it at all, it'll really help me get a break and then come back to work with a clear head and ready to dig in to what needs to be done.

MB: Hmmm . . . that's an interesting idea. Sort of a "work-free" zone?

LW: Somewhat, but not entirely. Remember, I'm not aiming for a schedule of leaving at 6 P.M. and not doing any work until I get back the next morning. What I'd like is to have those evening hours—say, from 7 P.M. until 11 P.M.—the time when I would check my voice mail and e-mail only once. If there was a real crisis or something that absolutely can't wait until the morning, we all have each other's home phone numbers and I could always be reached.

MB: And what about your basketball games?

LW: It's not just the basketball games. I'd just like to know there's at least one day during the week when I can get totally disengaged from work. No e-mail, no voice mail, no pages, no nothing—just a chance to have some real time off so I can pay complete attention to my personal and family life. If we could agree that Saturday is that "no-work" zone, that would still mean I'd be checking voice mail and e-mail every two to three hours on Sunday and, no doubt, would be pounding away on the laptop in my den doing other work on Sunday.

MB: That sounds fine from your perspective, Lee, but what about the effect on everyone else? What if some of *us* decide to work on Saturday and need some information from you?

LW: If it's really urgent and can't wait at least until Sunday, then you have my home phone number. But I'd hope that before anyone calls me, they'd stop to ask if there's real business necessity to do so. Also, since we've agreed that this nonstop work is a concern for all of us, maybe we want to consider having everyone come up with this kind of time plan.

MB: I can see it now. I'll send out a memo saying, "Effective immediately, thou shalt not work on Saturdays and thou shalt not expect replies to your e-mail or voice mail except in cases of national emergencies."

LW: Well, I guess that's one way to do it but it probably isn't the best way. All I'm saying is that it might be time for all of us to look at this issue, because you know as well as I do that we're all feeling squeezed. When was the last time *you* managed to get through a Saturday or Sunday without handling all your messages and being interrupted by your pager?

MB: It's been a *long* time. Lee, I can understand what you're saying and why you're saying it. No matter how much work we have to do, none of us should feel like it's illegal to take a break sometime and get reintroduced to our personal lives. In my case, as you know, I don't have a family so some of those issues you raised aren't important. But I sure could use a break in the action now and then.

LW: I'm glad you agree, Mary. I know the pressure you're under for these launches. I just think we'll all do a better job on them if we get a chance to get disengaged and disconnected for even a little while.

MB: You've given me a lot to think about, Lee. Not only as it applies to you but also to me and the rest of the department. Let me take a day or so to mull it over and I'll get back to you by Friday morning at the latest. I'm still sort of uncomfortable with saying that I can guarantee you won't have to be available and accessible during certain times—the reality is that we all face those demands, like it or not. However, I can see your side of things and why this is important to you, and in fact, to the rest of us as well.

LW: Thanks very much, Mary. I realize this is a difficult subject, and I wouldn't have brought it up unless I felt it was really important to me and to how I can do my best work for the company.

Instant Replay: What Happened, How It Happened, and Why

Let's scroll back up and analyze how this discussion went, and how it does—or doesn't—represent the kinds of conversations you might have with your boss or co-workers. Granted, it's a hypothetical conversation between two mythical characters, but it represents the real world because:

- The problems are typical;
- The characters responded as many or most (but not all) people would in real life;
- The resolution was positive yet tentative, and there were some loose ends to be handled later.

The biggest departure from real life was the exclusion of any discussion of access and availability during vacation or holiday periods. I left that out to keep the dialogue from getting even longer and more complex, and because for most people this process of setting boundaries has to begin in the context of the regular workweek. You're working more weeks than you're on vacation or holiday, so it makes sense to start with the workweeks.

There are three insights to be gained from this dialogue:

1. Lee: Calm, Prepared, and Didn't Take the Bait. Lee described the realizations about being absent from the bedtime-story reading and from the basketball court, as well as always having work on the mind, but didn't come across as being bitter, angry at Mary, or as making outrageous de-

mands. The problems were stated in terms that were meant to convey both their seriousness *and* an awareness of how they had to be solved in a way that met the business needs.

There were several times when Mary's retorts were a little cynical or emotional, and could have triggered a defensive or argumentative response from Lee—for example, when she said, "*You've* decided? Well, that's interesting. What did you have in mind—walking out of here at 4:30 every day and spending your weekends at the lake?" Although that may not have sounded all that bad to Lee, the response that came back to Mary was measured and positive.

THE LESSON: If you think through your message before the meeting, and do some practice or role-playing in which your "boss" tosses objections or remarks back at you and you get used to responding without getting angry, you'll have a more productive discussion. (See the final section of this chapter, titled "Handling the Zingers," for more tips on dealing with these objections or comebacks.)

2. Mary: The Firm Boss Versus the Empathetic Boss. We saw Mary vacillate between two ways of responding: she showed some understanding and empathy for Lee's situation and concerns, and even admitted that she had been experiencing the same things. But Mary also responded as a typical boss who herself was getting lots of pressure to produce on deadline, and who was perhaps a little shocked or offended that one of her staff would come in and ask for "time off."

THE LESSON: While some bosses are certainly all firmness and no empathy, and some are all empathy and no firmness, most are somewhere in the middle. If you make a reasonable case and have reasonable expectations for change, *and* show that you're still willing to carry your share of the workload, most managers will respond in a positive, problem-solving manner.

3. The Open Issues That Remain. This hypothetical dialogue left everything wrapped up in a pretty package at the end; although Mary said she wanted some time to think it over, we got the impression that Lee's case was well made and that the two of them were at, or very close to, a point of mutually satisfactory resolution. In real life, there could have been other issues to be handled, such as:

- How the co-workers would respond to Lee's plan—and what would happen if they all decided to do the same thing;
- What would happen the first time someone tried to reach Lee on the weekend and didn't get a response back until Monday morning;
- How Mary would explain things to *her* boss if he or she sent Lee an e-mail at 8 P.M. on an urgent matter and didn't hear back until the next morning;
- Whether Mary's assessment of Lee's performance and potential would drop because of Lee's request for tighter boundaries between work and personal time.

All of the above are the ripple effects of a conversation like this. It isn't enough for you to think about your own plan and how it will work out between you and your boss, co-worker, or key client with whom you have this discussion. You need to do a good deal of "what-if" thinking as part of your preparation—much in the same way that a good chess player always thinks a couple of moves ahead before picking up a piece to be moved.

Finally, keep in mind that this sample dialogue didn't include the kind of summary or recap that was suggested as Step 5 earlier in this chapter, or the reinforcement/recognition action suggested as Step 6. The recap was omitted here because the action plan was fairly simple and straightforward, and Lee had taken time to clarify as the conversation went along. The reinforcement step is, by definition, something that only happens after—perhaps considerably after—the actual conversation itself.

Handling the Zingers

A good part of my sometimes misspent youth was spent reading *MAD* magazine, a monthly compilation of satire, parody, and other assorted humor aimed mostly at the preadolescent and adolescent market but not without its appeal to adults.

One of my favorite parts was the "Snappy Answers to Stupid Questions" feature written and drawn by *MAD* veteran Al Jaffee. Here's an example that appears in *Completely MAD: A History of the Comic Book and Magazine* by Maria Reidelbach: A cartoon shows a line of people waiting at a ticket window, and a man approaches the last person in the queue. "Is this the end of the line?" he asks. The "snappy answers" shown are:

No, it's the beginning. We're all facing backwards!

No, it's the end of a freight train, and I'm the caboose!

No, it's a group of casual strollers, who, by some fan-
tastic coincidence, have come to stand one behind
the other at this one spot!

When Mary said, "*You've* decided? Well, that's interesting.
What did you have in mind—walking out of here at 4:30 every
day and spending your weekends at the lake?" I was sorely
tempted based on my *MAD* tutelage to have Lee reply, "Actually, I was planning on leaving at 5:00 but 4:30 sounds even
better. Thanks—I knew you'd understand!"

However, upon reflection I decided to keep the dialogue on
the straight and narrow—and you should, too if you get a
response that tempts you to come back with an equally cutting reply, unless you have another job already lined up and
want to go out in a blaze of glory.

As a final preparatory step, here are some of the comments
you might get in your real-life discussions when you're trying
to establish your time zones, and some suggested responses
that will keep the conversation on an even keel. I'll leave it to
you to imagine what those career-limiting "snappy answers"
might be:

IF YOU HEAR: "Who ever said that you're entitled to have
your nights and weekends off? Wake up, this is the Internet
age when time just doesn't slow down!"

YOU MIGHT REPLY: "Believe me, I know what we're up
against. Everything has to be done yesterday. But the problem
is, we're all running at that pace and we're starting to let
things fall between the cracks. I'm not looking to have my
nights and weekends off; that would be great but it's unrealistic today. All I'm saying is that I'd like to have us agree that
those periods are different from the normal workday Monday

through Friday. I don't want to escape from my responsibilities—I just want to be able to have a little more time for myself and be a little less compelled to be as responsive and available as I am all day long."

IF YOU HEAR: "Hey, I know it would be nice to simply get away from it all when you're on vacation. But you know how lean the staffing is here—I just can't afford to let anyone get completely out of touch for a few days, let alone a week or more."

YOU MIGHT REPLY: "No doubt about it—we have too much to do and too few people to do it, and I realize it's going to stay that way for a while. But that's exactly why I think it makes sense to have at least some time when we can get off that treadmill and let our brains take a rest. As it is, I came back from my last vacation more tired and, to be honest, more frustrated than I was when I left. It's just not a vacation when you're being paged several times a day and you're expected to check your voice mail morning, noon, and night. Maybe we can't get completely 'unplugged' but I'd like to have us agree that checking and responding to e-mail and voice mail only once a day on vacation is sufficient."

IF YOU HEAR: "Of *course* your pager goes off during the evening, and you're expected to check your e-mail at home at night—why do you think we spent all the money to give you that technology?"

YOU MIGHT REPLY: "I realize the company has made a huge investment in that stuff, and I wouldn't want to go back to the 'old days' without it for anything. But there comes a point when these things stop being productivity tools and start being millstones around our necks. If it's a really urgent problem or an emergency, by all means page me; otherwise, I'd like to suggest that we agree to strictly limit the use of pagers at night and check our e-mail at home once per evening. Otherwise, the technology that we all value becomes something that my family and I start to resent—and I'm not willing to let that happen if we can avoid it."

And last but not least, the ultimate zinger:

IF YOU HEAR: "Well, if you aren't willing to carry your share of the load and be a team player, I guess I'll have to start looking for someone who is."

YOU MIGHT REPLY: "I'll be honest—that statement bothers me. I think you've seen over the last six months that I'm perfectly willing to pitch in and work the kinds of hours we all have in order to stay on schedule. There comes a point, however, when work is no longer something that I do as part of my life—it becomes *all* of my life, and that's not acceptable. If you aren't satisfied with my performance in general, then we need to talk about that because I enjoy working here and want to be sure you're getting what you need from me. But I'd like you to realize that in the process of doing what's expected, I feel like I've lost all separation between work and my personal life—and it's time to start drawing some boundaries between the two. Let's see if we can't agree on how to do that and still make sure I'm supporting the team and the company."

As you may have felt when you read Lee and Mary's conversation, it's always easier to come back with these kinds of clear, calm, and assertive responses when you're not engaged in the conversation yourself. It's the same as being in the stands at a sporting event and watching how the players are performing—the benefit of hindsight and oversight is undeniable.

My goal, though, is to help and encourage you to learn how you can come up with these more positive responses even when you're involved in the discussion yourself. If you realize how they can help defuse what might otherwise become a tough situation and can help you achieve your goals, you'll be able to draw on your resources and handle these and similar "zingers" with the right attitude and reactions.

Neither you nor I can control how your customers, co-workers, or boss will handle their end of the conversation; that's why this chapter has put so much emphasis on what you can do to help that conversation along. The next chapter looks at the other side of the process: what you can do if *you're* the boss.

CHAPTER 7

WHAT TO DO IF YOU'RE THE BOSS

In a perfect work world, this chapter would be superfluous because employers would have long ago understood the potential problems that can occur when people lose the boundary between work and life and would have taken steps to prevent those problems. Someone in a walnut-paneled corner office would have issued an edict saying, "Our employees *are* entitled to have a life outside of work!" Doors on the office would be locked at 6 P.M. and wouldn't open again until 7 A.M., and e-mail and voice mail systems would always be down for maintenance from 8 P.M. Friday until 8 P.M. Sunday.

Vacations and holidays would be sacrosanct; no longer would anyone be expected or even encouraged to pack a laptop, pager, or cell phone along with vacation gear. And, most important, life in the organization would go on with no problems at all.

But Until Hell Freezes Over . . .

If you want to stick around for that happily-ever-after scenario to become reality you're going to have a long wait. Meantime, we all have to deal with the real world. It is a world in which precious few employers to date have even acknowledged this issue of disappearing boundaries and even fewer have taken any steps to do anything about it. Will that change in time? Perhaps so. Will it change sooner rather than later? Probably not.

Chapters 4 through 6 were written for people who are dealing with the kinds of time and work-life boundary issues this book addresses. The assumption was that the individual who faces these challenges is in the best position to find solutions for them, and that's still a valid assumption. In this chapter, though, we'll change viewpoints and think about ways in which managers can at the very least reinforce the attempts by their staff to make these changes, and at best can stimulate their staff to give some thought to the need for clearer boundaries between work and life. This process might lead to changes the manager can then encourage and reinforce.

(Managers are, of course, employees themselves, and as such were also the focus of the preceding four chapters. In this chapter we'll concentrate on managers as managers and how they affect the boundary-setting behavior of *their* employees.)

The Manager's Action Spectrum

If you're the boss and it seems sensible to you to be mindful of these boundary issues, you have to walk a fine line between helping your employees with these issues and actively encouraging, or even requiring, that they make some changes. In my view, it is just as unproductive for a manager to require employees to check their voice mail three times a day on weekends as it is to mandate that they don't check it at all on weekends. Either extreme brings its own set of problems.

One way for you to get past this dilemma is to view your possible actions along a spectrum that includes a range of steps you can take:

X————————X———————X——————————X
Decriminalizing Enabling Encouraging Mandating

Let's consider your options on this spectrum:

Decriminalizing means that you won't berate, punish, intimidate, embarrass, or otherwise do anything even re-motely negative if one of your employees decides to set some firmer (and reasonable) boundaries between work and per-sonal time. In many organizations, there are certain kinds of "criminal" behaviors that, while not illegal in a literal sense, are known in the corporate culture to be highly risky and thus ill advised. These actions might not even be specifically pro-scribed by the corporate policies manual but might as well be.

For example, in some organizations it is perceived as "illegal" to:

- Argue with a senior manager in a meeting or other open setting;
- Show up more than five minutes late for a meeting;
- Have more than one or two drinks at a company-sponsored social event;
- Use obscene or vulgar language in public.

Behaviors like these, no matter how justified they might have been, help make up the norms of the organization, usually have long roots and may have been responsible for a key element of the lore—for example, "I remember back in 1991 when Tony Wilson stood up at a division meeting and told the vice president that his financial projections were incorrect. Poor old Tony was out on the street within a week—and nobody ever spoke up to that VP again."

Similarly, a person might have been thought to be a "corporate criminal" if he or she chose not to carry a pager on weekends or take a laptop on a family trip. When we talk about how a manager might decriminalize this kind of behavior, we're saying that the manager gets the word out—often explicitly—that these behaviors are no longer cause for fear and possible retribution or punishment.

That doesn't mean the behaviors will change overnight, but at least the organization begins to realize that they aren't cause for being beheaded in the company cafeteria at high noon. This is obviously the most limited action you can take; it's not likely to create or stimulate much change but at least it gets the word out that you are willing to *accept* changes if your staff so chooses.

Enabling means that the manager not only makes the new behaviors safer, but goes the next step and does a few things to make it easier for employees to use them. The manager doesn't take an activist stance but lets it be known that *if* the employees want to make some changes, the manager will be receptive to hearing about them and will do what he or she can, within reason, to support the changes.

Some of the things managers can do to *enable* employee efforts to set up the three-zones model include:

- Being available to discuss the ways in which the employee wants to implement these changes;
- Being willing to suggest alternative strategies and to intervene on the employee's behalf (upon request only) with other staff members or other departments;
- Agreeing to honor the employee's requests for the use of the "mid-duty" and "off duty" time zones as long as they don't interfere with the business and mission of the department;
- Being quick to provide feedback to the employee if the manager sees (or hears about) problems being caused by the employee's use of the three time zones.

"Enabling" in this context means to help, facilitate, or empower; it does not mean that the manager will be expected to initiate or unilaterally act on the employee's behalf. As such, it is a very subtle kind of support—more than just removing the sanction of "criminality" but less than taking an activist role toward or for employees.

Encouraging moves the manager farther along this spectrum; it involves some outreach initiated by the manager because he or she believes in the value of establishing clearer boundaries between work and life. The manager who begins to actively encourage will be most successful if his or her motives are balanced between what's right for the organization and for the people. If the motivation is purely altruistic or if the potential consequences for the organization aren't considered, this kind of encouragement is likely to produce problems, not progress.

A manager might decide to move toward the "encouraging" point on the spectrum for many reasons, including:

- Noticing that employees are fatigued and frustrated, and don't seem to return to work in the morning or after a weekend any more rested or relaxed than when they left;
- Experiencing employee turnover (or hearing about it in other departments) when the stated cause is something like "We just can't get a breather around here";
- Noticing that quality and comprehensiveness are being sacrificed in the name of speed and responsiveness; for example, e-mail sent in the late afternoon that might benefit from a more thoughtful reaction is answered with a brief and choppy reply at 9 P.M.—almost as if the recipient decided it was better to respond fast than to respond well;
- Noticing that voice mail and e-mail messages have date and time stamps* indicating that the sender was working considerably beyond what most people would consider normal hours—even allowing for today's longer workweeks.

There's one more reason managers might choose to actively encourage some boundary setting: their own beliefs about the fundamental sense of equity and fairness that should exist in a modern organization. It may seem that a manager who encourages employees to preserve some more time for them-

---

* Be sure you don't infer too much from these date and time stamps. Depending on how your corporate voice and data networks operate, the dates and times on messages may not reflect the local time when and where the sender sent them. A message with a time stamp of 11 P.M. might actually have been sent at 8 P.M. in the time zone where the sender was located.

selves is looking a gift horse in the mouth, given today's push to do everything faster.

But I believe there is a small yet growing number of managers today who understand that faster is better only in the short term, and that the terms of employment do not include near-unlimited access to the employee's intellectual capacity. These managers also realize that employees can only sustain the pace of a sprinter for just so long before they tire and burn out. The managers who encourage staff to pace themselves are not being benevolent as much as they are being pragmatic. The sprinters who work very long hours and then burn out are of no value to an organization that's trying to sustain itself for the future.

Mandating is the last position on the spectrum; in my view it is often counterproductive and even dangerous. Managers who issue fiats declaring that "you are not to check your voice mail or e-mail on weekends or vacations" or "I don't want anyone staying in the office past 7 P.M." are not likely to get the results—and respect—they might be expecting.

This might seem ironic. What could be wrong with telling employees that you *don't* want them to work all kinds of long and disruptive hours? Isn't that a sign of a caring, worker-friendly style of management that managers are supposed to practice? Managers might view this anti-edict admonition as the ultimate "damned if you do—damned if you don't" situation. "First you tell me it's wrong to expect my people to work all hours of the day and night," the manager might think, "and then you tell me it's wrong if I tell them *not* to do that!"

To those managers, I simply say, "Relax, and think before you act." This is another case where the extreme positions are not as helpful as the admittedly more difficult middle ground. Having expectations about nonstop work is wrong, but here are some reasons why declaring a rule about preventing it is equally wrong:

1. Few people want to be told that they can't do to themselves something that most people would judge to be harmful, even if they agree it's harmful. Witness the reactions so many people have about why they continue to smoke, don't wear seat belts, remain dangerously overweight, and so on. "It's my life and I'll take my chances" is the typical reaction, as incomprehensible as you or I may find it.

2. Something that is "bad," "wrong," or "not advised" in the general case may be just the opposite in specific situations. This book is about the problems that can arise when someone loses the boundary between work time and personal time, and allows the former to consume much of the latter. The fact that most people would see that as problematic does not mean that everyone does—and as I write these words I remind myself about that distinction as much as I urge you to keep it in mind.

If you have an employee who willingly stays up until midnight doing work, spends a bright, sunny Saturday afternoon answering e-mail, and willingly takes a cell phone and laptop on vacation—*and* does not show any signs of diminished performance, satisfaction, or ability to work with others—it's risky for you to step in and label that behavior as wrong and thus something that should be stopped.

3. A trendy term to describe today's secret for meeting consumer expectations is "mass customization"—an oxymoron if ever there was one, but a useful one nonetheless. For example, if I'm a clothing manufacturer and I can mass-

produce blue jeans and at the same time profitably create a somewhat customized pair for you, I've achieved the best of both worlds.

A manager needs to apply this same "mass customization" concept to managing today—and not just around issues of time and technology use. Today's workforce is increasingly diverse and differentiated, and the notion that one management style fits all is completely outdated. This makes life more complicated for managers, but that just goes with the job title these days. As long as any single employee's time use is not creating problems for others and is not jeopardizing the amount or quality of his or her long-term contributions, the manager has no grounds for imposing work-life time boundaries that apply universally to everyone.

This doesn't mean you can't decide as a manager to implement some very specific and selective rules that act as a *framework* or parameter within which each employee can still create his or her own schedule and approach to the three time zones. For example, you can tell your staff:

- While the team is obligated to respond during the work week to pages from each other within 30 minutes, that increases to two hours on the weekend and pages should only be sent if there is a clear business necessity to contact the person within two hours.
- The decision to check voice mail and e-mail while on holiday or vacation time is a personal one; any employees who decide not to do so should make that clear to their co-workers. You should also tell the staff about your own decision on this issue. You can also remind your staff

about the purpose of vacations, and that you expect people to return from them refreshed, recharged, and ready to jump back into the job with lots of energy.

- You may be at times be tempted to tell people who send or respond to voice mail and e-mail at, say, 11 P.M. that they should turn it off and go to sleep. Instead, your position is that such behavior is something you don't want to encourage or reinforce, and it's not something you're going to reward when it comes time for performance reviews and salary/bonus consideration. If they choose to work those hours, they should understand it *is* a choice and not an implied or expressed obligation.

The Power of Being a Model

Managers, human resources staffs, and boards of directors can write all the policies, mission statements, and other treatises they want, but none of those has the power to influence behavior that role modeling does. It's fine to say, "Do as I say (or as our policies say), not as I do" to your staff, but the reality is that they'll do as you do almost no matter what you say.

It's no secret that astute employees learn to look to their bosses to help figure out what to do and not do. Even if they don't agree with everything the boss does, they at least realize there might be some risk in straying too far from the model set by the boss. The more open-minded and enlightened the manager, the more he or she accepts, and even welcomes, staff behavior that's different as long as it's not destructive. But down deep, I think we all like it when someone does what we do. Following that model can be the most blatant form of pandering—but it's still flattering.

As manager, you have an opportunity to make it easier for your staff members who are trying to establish some work-personal time boundaries by showing them how you do the same thing. There's no need to put yourself up on a pedestal or give the impression that your approach to the three-zones time model is ideal; all you need to do is demonstrate (by words and actions) that it is *legitimate and acceptable* to live by that model as long as it doesn't create significant business problems.

Some of the ways you can lead this change process *without* imposing it on your staff are to:

- Establish and Explain Your Three-Zones Model. Take the time to figure out what your "on duty," "mid-duty" and "off duty" hours are and discuss them at a staff meeting. Talk about the thinking that went into the process and why you decided to set up the boundaries in general. Also, be sure to define for your staff what they can expect in terms of response and access to you during your "mid-duty" times in particular.
- Use Technology to "Cheat." Many corporate e-mail and voice mail systems allow for a delayed-delivery option. This means you can record a voice message or type out an e-mail and then instruct the system not to deliver it to the recipient's mailbox until hours, or possibly even days, later. If you can't avoid the urge to send out those messages during what would otherwise be your "off duty" time, you can take advantage of this delayed-delivery fea-

ture so those messages don't arrive until a more reasonable time.

- Decide How You're Going to Handle Vacations and Holidays. It's one thing to have to work late at night at home, or to answer e-mail on the weekend—it's quite another to have to check voice mail a few times a day when you're on a long-awaited vacation. The good news about moving up the organizational ladder is that you have more responsibility, more challenge, and more compensation; the bad news is that you have less control of your time and schedule. But even if you are absolutely required to be accessible to your management during vacation, that doesn't mean that you have to be accessible to—or have access to—your staff.

- Don't Expect More Than *You* Can Accept. We can generalize from that last point about the difference between your choices about the three zones versus the choices your staff makes. It's important to make sure you don't expect more of your staff than you are willing to live with yourself—and this doesn't apply only to vacations and holidays.

- Deal with the Patterns, Not the Incidents. If you get an occasional e-mail sent at midnight from one of your staff, there's no need to jump on that person for working too late. But if you see a pattern of long and late hours, and weekend work, I think you have the opportunity and the responsibility to discuss it with the person. The tone of the discussion should be, "I've noticed you've been working pretty late just about every night for the last few weeks, judging by your e-mail. That's certainly your option. I just want to see if there's anything going on here that's causing you to put in those hours and whether it's a problem for you." That's a problem-solving approach, and it's much more likely to be welcomed than if you start off with "What the heck are you doing up and working at midnight just about every night? Get some sleep—and get a life!"

- Attention Conveys Importance. One of my past managers used to say that "management *expects* what management *inspects*." In other words, the best way to figure out what's important to your boss (i.e., expects) is to observe what the boss asks about (i.e., inspects) on the first day back after vacation, or at weekly staff meetings, or any other time when the boss has an opportunity to talk with the full staff or with each person one-on-one.

The simple act of asking about something signals that it's on your mind and your radar screen. For example, if you ask on a Monday morning, "How was your weekend? What did you do with the family?" or "Did you get a chance to go out hiking like you said you were going to?" those questions are subtle but powerful ways of communicating that you are interested in your employees' lives—not just their work lives.

The Risks of Unintentional Reinforcement

There's another aspect of being a role model: the ways in which you unknowingly and unintentionally send a signal that encourages the kind of behavior that you and your employees might be trying to change.

A few years ago, I was working with a company for which the issue of long work hours and, in particular, being in the office on weekends was something its executives were trying to change. Top management had held meetings to discuss it, considered (but decided against) locking the building to prevent weekend access, and went as far as to agree among themselves that they would leave the office no later than 7 P.M. each day and avoid coming in on weekends. So far, so good: they were really sincere in trying to change the work patterns, which was especially difficult since this was a high-tech startup company.

I was reviewing progress with my client one Monday afternoon and she told me that a recent event had all but undone those previous efforts. They had a divisionwide, all-level staff meeting that morning, and near the end of the meeting the vice president of operations was making his report. At the end of the report, he happened to mention that he was in the office Saturday to pick up some papers, and noticed that two of his engineers were at their desks working. "With a big smile on his face," my client told me, "the VP said, 'Good to see those guys here on a Saturday afternoon—it shows they're really pitching in to help us move ahead.' I couldn't believe it—with that one sentence he set us back six months."

Let's give that VP the benefit of the doubt and say that he wasn't trying to explicitly reward or praise those two engineers. It just slipped out during the staff meeting, but it did so in a way that telegraphed to everyone attending how *it appeared* he really felt about cutting back on work hours. Actually, I don't know how the VP really felt—I'm just saying that his little speech created the perception that he felt long hours and weekend work in the office were praiseworthy.

That one slip didn't really set the effort to cut back hours by six months, but that was the fear of my client. She correctly understood that the VP's statement—not to mention the fact that he said *he* was in the office on Saturday—would likely have a powerful effect. Similarly, you need to be aware of the things you do or say that *completely unintentionally* send a very different message than you are otherwise trying to send.

You and Your Peer Managers

Just as employees at all levels look up to their boss and his or her boss for cues and clues about how to behave, managers look across the organization to see how other managers are acting, for two reasons. Few people want to be the odd person out, and managers generally know how important it is to act with unity and present a consistent story to the organization.

So, what do you do if you want to set up a three-zones model with a reasonable amount of "mid-duty" and "off duty" time for yourself and the others don't? Or what happens if the opposite occurs: other managers are doing a good job preserving some personal time for themselves but *you're* the one in the office on the weekends and sending e-mail from your cabin in the mountains while you're vacationing? You have three choices:

1. Ignore It. Unless you're getting a lot of pressure from above for all managers to act uniformly in this regard, there may be no need to concern yourself with what other managers do. This is no different from any other area of managerial action; you look to your peers to see what they're doing and then change (or not) based on what makes the most

sense to you. If you've decided that clearer time boundaries and more "mid-duty" and "off duty" time are desirable and feasible for you, then you'll do it. And if you want to keep a majority of your 168 hours blocked off for "on duty" and "mid-duty" time, that's what you'll do.

2. Change Yourself. In my corporate days there were times I changed the most based on the model being set by managers I liked the most—and in some cases by managers I liked the least. It's a sign of maturity, flexibility—or political astuteness—to see what your peers are doing and use that information to help shape your own actions.

Because we're talking about some important personal choices here, and not whether you should use a certain version of spreadsheet software, you are more likely to scan your periphery to see what many managers are doing. If their actions, and the results they get, are appealing to you, perhaps it's time to follow their lead.

3. Change the Others. Do you really believe that the organization in general would benefit from a work culture in which people were able to preserve a bit more personal time for themselves? Do you think, or have evidence that, newer or younger employees are heading for the exits because they don't like being on an 80-hour-a-week treadmill? If so, maybe your strategy with your peers is to try to influence their behavior and, by extension, that of their staff.

This can be tricky business, however. You may be accused of being everything from an idealistic crusader who wants to be nice to everyone, to an unrealistic and selfish hedonist who would rather take the kids to the playground on a Sunday afternoon than stay home and revise the marketing plan. Issues about how we spend our time are about much more than who stays later than whom in the office or who answers the cell phone while on vacation. Those are only proxy measures for deeper questions about the role of work in our lives, and the extent to which we are, or should be, willing to make short-term sacrifices for long-term gains. I'm not saying you shouldn't try to influence your peers if that's what you believe is right; I would just caution you to expect everything from appreciation to highly personal criticisms.

You and *Your* Boss

Last, let's consider what all of this means for the relationship between you and your boss. I noted at the beginning of the chapter that previous chapters covered your own decision making about time and life as an employee and that this chapter would change the focus to your supervisory role. Now it's time to bring those two perspectives together.

You have seen in this chapter that the actions you take as a manager are conditioned by the choices you make about your own use of time and your willingness to be accessible and available outside of normal working hours. As with any employee, those choices are the starting point for discussions with your manager. Those discussions get a little more complicated when your boss is thinking not only about how your choices and preferences affect you and your performance, but also how they affect the model you set and the expectations you have for your own staff.

This isn't much different from how your manager manages you relative to other issues, for example, attendance and timeliness. Your boss can't be any more (or less) liberal with how your attendance and timeliness are treated than he or she expects you to be with your own employees. Thus, it might be hard for your boss to accept the idea that you'll exempt your employees from carrying a pager or checking voice mail while on vacation if you yourself aren't similarly excused.

On the other hand, your boss might say, "Look, if you think you can get your job done without being in touch with your people while they're on vacation, that's your choice. Just don't expect the same treatment from me." This is an obvious clue that you and your boss might have some serious talking to do. That sample response from the boss carries a lot of hidden messages about expectations for your own performance, your managerial competence, and the extent to which you're going to be able to carve out some real "off duty" time during vacation if you choose to do so.

It's impossible to suggest how you should handle this kind of disconnect between what you believe in for yourself and your staff versus what is being expected for you. Suffice it to say that you'll need to draw on all your tact, patience, and logical reasoning skill to reconcile those two positions. I'll leave you with the thought that it's very difficult for most people to manage *up* one way and manage *down* a different way; it isn't long before that kind of split managerial personality begins to take its toll on everyone involved.

CHAPTER 8

WHAT'S AHEAD—AND WHAT IT MEANS
FOR YOUR "TURN IT OFF" PROSPECTS

It's almost impossible to make specific projections about trends in work, workplaces, and technology. The more I read about how blindingly fast all three (especially technology) are changing, the more I realize that we can only hope to identify the general themes and directions.

Instead, I'll glance into the future as best I can and concentrate on the overall trends and not the specific changes. In doing so, I'm reminded of a suitable admonition from Paul Saffo of the Institute for the Future: "Never mistake a clear view for a short distance." I asked Paul about the origin of this statement, and he said, "I first heard it from an old rancher where I lived as a child. For me, it nicely expresses the pattern we see again and again in technology—something seems so obvious that it should happen immediately, but then takes forever to arrive."

This is good advice for all of us these days, since there are many technology developments that we've been anticipating and that have been promised to us for a long time (such as movies on demand, wall-size displays, high-quality and low-cost desktop videoconferencing). Given the explosive pace of technology development, it seems *so* logical to expect that we'd have these and more available today, but they aren't quite here yet.

After we take that look into the future, I'll then give you some guidelines about factors that will predict your own ability to "turn it off." These factors will let you make the bridge between my glimpse ahead and the specifics of how your own work schedule and style will be affected by the trends that I'll be discussing.

Coming Full Circle

I'll try to stay away from the kinds of predictions that are based on what *should* happen if everything goes right and instead will focus on what is *very likely* to happen based on known technologies and business trends. The best way to look into the future is to return to the three factors identified in Chapter 1 that form the foundation of this book:

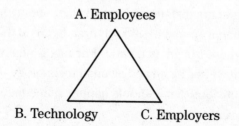

A. Employees: Do It All, Want It All, Have It All

As we look at the likely employee response to what will happen around them, I believe the driving theme will be simple: employers will be considered guilty until proven innocent in the eyes of employees whose tolerance for less-than-desirable work or working conditions will reach an all-time low. The use, or misuse, of technology is an important component of those working conditions but far from the only one.

A recent magazine ad focused this issue very clearly for me. IntraLinks Inc., which provides "Internet-based services to manage business-critical communications," has as its advertising theme, and splash page on its Web site <www.intra links.com>, the trademarked phrase "Is it work if you love it?" That caught my eye the first time I read it and really made me think about the way most of us experience what we do for the 2,000 to 3,000 hours a year we spend at work, wherever and whatever that may be.

That deceptively simple question in the Intralinks ad is actually a philosophical teaser because it forces us to start thinking about what we expect from and are willing to put up with in our work and our jobs. The implied message is that "work" connotes boredom, drudgery, displeasure, and pain and that if you love what you're doing then it simply *can't* be "work." My sense is that today's workforce will become increasingly intolerant of work if it means boredom, drudgery, displeasure, and mental stress. This doesn't imply that people won't be willing to work hard or do something they don't like; it means they just won't put up with a job in which those kinds of negatives are characteristic.

You may be thinking, "So what—what's new about that? There's nothing new about someone wanting to leave a job that causes them to be consistently tired, angry, or frustrated." That's true—people don't tend to stay in jobs that they despise. What's new is that the *threshold* for when the person says, "That's enough—I can't take it. I'm outta here!" will be much lower than before. In other words, it will take much less to push someone out the door and into the arms of another (people-hungry) employer, or startup, or entrepreneurial opportunity.

Why will this be true? Three reasons come to mind:

1. "Get Rich Quick?" No—"Get Rich *Now*!" You've seen the same survey results I have: a high proportion of today's college students (from 50 to 75 percent, in reports I've seen) expect to become millionaires—and it won't be when they're sitting around in rocking chairs. The dot-com mania and wild run-up of high-tech stocks in the late 1990s have conditioned people to believe that exceptional wealth is no longer exceptional. We might disagree with that expectation or feel that it is symptomatic of a serious underlying problem, but the fact remains that the expectation is there and it *will* drive the decision making of younger employees. I don't think they're going to tolerate a work environment that robs them of their personal lives.

2. "Golden Handcuffs" Don't Work. Most people in the workforce today in their 40s or 50s have been conditioned to equate longevity with retirement income and/or access to stock options. If you want those goodies you have to stay on the payroll for at least five years and in many cases ten years. While that might have seemed like a long time, it was how the game was played; if you left sooner you risked losing some or

all of those benefits. And if you left for another employer, you would likely have to start at the bottom of the vacation-entitlement ladder because you no longer had the years of service that gave you that extra week or two of paid vacation.

That way of thinking is almost completely alien for today's workers in their 20s and (at least early) 30s. They are much less motivated to do something today in order to get a benefit 10 or 20 years later, and they are also often able to get the same kinds of benefits on day one with a new employer, especially if their skills are in demand. We're living in a time when signing bonuses and other up-front perks are almost as common and lucrative in the business world as they are in the sports world. If that's so, why on earth would an employee tolerate annoying or aggravating working conditions for longer than, say, a few months? This doesn't mean employers can underpay their new hires and give them lots of schedule flexibility instead. It means that these students won't be as swayed by a job offering high monetary benefits at the cost of quality of life.

3. Yesterday a Stigma—Today a Badge of Honor. It used to be a curse to be labeled as a "job-hopper"; the applicant whose work history showed short tenures and multiple employers was suspect and had a hard time being hired. Today, it's almost exactly the opposite. Many employers specifically want to avoid applicants who are too stable and have spent long periods with one or two employers. That kind of employment record is perceived as a sign that the person isn't aggressive enough, isn't skilled enough to be in demand by lots of companies, and will bring the perspective of only one or two companies instead of six to ten. Assuming that's true, what could possibly motivate an employee to "stick it

out" in an undesirable job for longer than a few months—let alone a few years?

These changing employee preferences and tolerance levels are directly related to the question of boundary-setting and time allocation between work and the rest of life. There are and will be plenty of workers who will put in long hours and give up their weekends and perhaps even vacations for jobs and causes in which they believe. But this will *only* happen if it is *their own* decision to spend their time and their lives this way. Managerial imposition of (or managerial endorsement of customer expectations for) those terms of employment just won't work.

But if the Economy Takes a Nose Dive?

I think it's unlikely that we'll see a major economic downturn or prolonged recession in the near term. I hope I haven't been proven wrong by the time you read this. I remain optimistic, yet at the same time I can't ignore the concerns of others who assert that the low part of the economic cycle is bound to revisit our economy.

Many of today's employees, especially those in their 20s, have become spoiled—I can't think of any other way to describe it. They are enjoying a level of compensation, benefits, and employer willingness to cater to (almost) their every need such as was never seen in the past. This isn't just flextime and fitness centers we're talking about—it's massage therapy at your desk, free lunches prepared by gourmet chefs, and free use of a concierge service that will do just about anything legal and moral. These are services open to *all* the office workers in the firms that offer them, not just to the select few top executives.

An employer's willingness to extend this kind of largess is a good proxy measure for its willingness to be responsive to employee requests for better boundary setting between work and personal time. In a weak economy with high unemployment, an employee who proposed to turn off the pager on weekends, for example, would probably be urged to turn on the PC and update his or her resumé. Today, and in the foreseeable future especially in the technology-based jobs, I believe these employees are more likely to be coddled. That's why we can expect employees to continue raising these issues—as well they should, because once these new work patterns are established it will be hard (though certainly not impossible) for employers to revert back to expectations for anytime-anywhere work.

B. Technology: Smaller, Faster, Cheaper, Better

We will continue to see more vendor offerings of products and services that enable, if not encourage, mobile work at virtually any time and in virtually any location. Some of the equipment providers are finding intriguing ways to craft a message that blends mobility with flexibility and "freedom of choice," as seen in Toshiba's brand-awareness campaign for its line of laptops. The campaign "encourages people to use today's technologies to choose when, where and how they work and, as a result, realize a more productive and satisfying work experience," says Toshiba.

In general, it's a no-brainer to predict that technology will become even smaller, faster, and cheaper. For the following reasons, whether or not it will definitely become *better* remains an open question in my mind:

1. Huge Opportunities for Tiny Fingers. We have reached the point where mobility is the watchword and portability is limited only by the strength of our vision (to read tiny characters on tiny screens) and the size and dexterity of our fingers (to use tiny keyboards or to write with a stylus on tiny screens). Depending on how quickly we have truly functional voice recognition—a technology about which I continue to be skeptical—the tiny-fingers problem might eventually disappear.

2. Multi-Function, Multi-Location Devices. Cell phones are morphing into communications devices capable of sending and receiving text messages and surfing the Web, among other things. Text messaging units smaller than a deck of cards give you e-mail contact without a laptop and allow you to be reachable where it would be inappropriate to use a cell phone. Telecommunications providers are racing to beef up their wireless networks—and cell phone vendors their equipment—to all mobile access to much more than the rudimentary, stripped-down Web pages that could be viewed by early models.

If you prefer to work while in your car, you're not going to escape this technology juggernaut. We're turning our cars into mobile workstations; it's entirely possible that your car may be almost as well equipped to do work in 2003 as your desk was in 1993, and probably more so. Automakers including General Motors and Ford are developing prototypes of dashboard units that give drivers access to their corporate networks and to the Internet in general.

3. Bandwidth Will Still Dominate. Despite the wonderful developments we've seen and will see in hardware, the biggest changes in the future will come from the explosion of broadband access. Dial-up access by modem and analog phone line is likely to fade off in the sunset, to be replaced by high-speed access over one or another kind of digital lines or even satellite. Hotels are rushing to install these lines in business-traveler guest rooms, residential neighborhoods are being increasingly well blanketed with DSL capability and/or cable modem access, and there are some interesting wireless solutions on the horizon.

In a way, this trend concerns me. As long as a noticeable and significant speed gap exists between what I can do in the office versus what I can do from my home or other remote sites, there's a convenience barrier. I am effectively discouraged from doing all but the most simple work away from the office because anything more complex (that would require or at least benefit from faster access) goes too slowly. But if my access at home, or in a hotel room or elsewhere away from the office, approximates what I'm accustomed to in the office, there's no longer any technical disincentive to extending the workday, or workweek, away from the office.

The Reach of Technology Creates
Workplaces Everywhere

I'm not sure you'll be able to find many places where you can truly get away from work—or at least get away from the capability to do work. From ski lodges to cruise ships, and from airplanes to cars, it seems that workstations are popping up just about everywhere; you'll find a list of some of these in Chapter 9.

You might look at those examples and be excited because it means you'll have more flexibility to integrate work with your personal time and thus be less constrained by the traditional do-your-office-work-in-the-office model. Or you might look at them and be dismayed because it means you'll find it harder and harder to escape the visual cues and clues that remind you of how much work is on your to-do list, and how opportune it would be to tackle some of it in between the evening show and the midnight brunch on your next cruise, for example.

No matter what your viewpoint, it is undeniable that there will simply be more places where you can do more work, and many of them will be equipped with the kind of telecommunications access and equipment that will make them virtually indistinguishable from your regular office. I would argue that this trend will introduce new challenges for people who want to maintain some separation between work and the rest of their lives. It's as if someone trying to lose a little weight wakes up one morning to find a brand-new donut shop and ice cream store on one side of his or her house and three fast-food restaurants on the other side. Willpower works up to a point, but it's sorely tested when you're surrounded by temptation.

But—Perhaps *Too* Many Workplaces?

Just as we are surrounding ourselves with Internet access and all the rest, it's also possible that we'll face a "technology backlash" as people become overwhelmed by all that connectivity. Tod Maffin, a technology futurist in Vancouver, British Columbia, has observed that "the steady integration of e-business into aspects of business where humans used to intervene will cause us to increasingly, quietly rebel against technology periodically. The telco's dream of letting people 'be connected any time, any place' will not always mean a better life. The more the workplace gets wired, the less we'll want our homes to be. One of the most popular vacation destinations in the next decade will be spots that guarantee no cell phone coverage." Travel experts are predicting that interest in "no-tech" getaways will boom as, in the words of one writer, "detox centers for the chronically wired."

It would be the ultimate irony if all the hotels, resorts, cruise ships, and other travel and vacation venues that are rushing to install all the latest tools for connectivity find that their most harried and work-obsessed guests start shunning the tools and lie out by the pools instead.

This "no-tech" trend, if it is one, may be fed by nothing more than consumer and customer frustration; the annoyance levels with intrusive cell phones, for example, keep rising. At least one restaurant owner has had enough. Ed Moose, who owns a San Francisco restaurant named Moose's, banned cell phones in his establishment. His restaurant now has little signs on the tables that show a picture of a moose talking on the phone with the words "No cellular phones please."

Whether or not these gentle hints, or the individual efforts by restaurant owners, theaters, concert halls, and other public places, will pay off has yet to be seen. If voluntary compliance doesn't solve the problem, there's at least one technical solution: C-Guard, from NetLine Communications Technologies. This "cellular firewall" is described on the company's Web site as "a jammer device that transmits low power radio signals, which cut off communications between cellular handsets and cellular base stations. The jamming effect can be digitally controlled to form quiet zones in confined places." (If this is a response to technology backlash, there's *another* backlash building against C-Guard who assert that the use of the product is a violation of First Amendment freedom-of-speech rights. I won't touch that issue with a 50-foot cellular antenna pole.)

As we look ahead, then, we see a curious paradox developing: technology that is more robust, more available, less expensive, and easier to use—set against a backdrop of slowly growing resentment about its use. For now, the pro-technology forces seem to be prevailing, and that means the possibilities for anytime-anywhere work will keep multiplying.

C. Employers: Downsizing, Squeezing, Globalizing, Speeding Up

Short of a monumental stock market crash (heaven forbid), the election of a bevy of isolationist presidents, premiers, and prime ministers around the world (perish the thought), or a return to the staffing levels and pace of corporate life of the 1980s (wishful thinking), I can't imagine what would cause a major slowdown, let alone a reversal, in the trends driving employer change—with one exception, which I'll note shortly.

The Internet is speeding us toward marketplaces that are truly national and in many cases global. Corporate purchasing practices have shifted from suppliers trying to build relationships with purchasing agents to suppliers who have to bid openly against each other on auction sites for business that previously might have been almost guaranteed. Shareholders have become accustomed to seeing stock prices rise in direct proportion to layoff announcements. Most important, we have seen global consolidation in major industries that a few years ago would have been inconceivable—and shows no signs of slowing down.

This consolidation offers all kinds of synergies and benefits, or so say the CEOs who make the deals. But it also creates a frightening game of musical chairs in which employees of the soon-to-be-combined companies find themselves scurrying to secure one of a quickly shrinking number of jobs.

I'm not qualified to assess whether this consolidation trend is good or bad. My interest is in the *effects* of the consolidation—and in my view, they include an almost relentless process of trimming payrolls in the name of building the enterprise's value. In that kind of environment, the typical employee has considerably less leverage and clout than in, say, a fast-growth company in a field like technology or biotech. This means the employees in those firms that consolidate are, all else being equal, going to feel more pressure to "do more with less" and at the same time have less of a chance to influence work hours and boundary setting.

The Coming Employee Backlash

Now, about the exception to all this. I've made reference to this in the "Employees" section previously but at this point will suggest that employers' ability to get away with a "do more with less" corporate mind-set will be limited by growing employee backlash against it. This backlash is relatively new and as yet not widespread. But I believe there will be fewer employers who will be able to treat their workers the way many were squeezed, stretched, and overworked in the late 1990s and into this decade.

There are two important distinctions between the work environment in a growing startup where the employees willingly put in outrageously long hours and sleep under their desks, and the environment in an old-line organization that is desperately trying to drive out costs and drive up productivity and sales in order to be able to compete with those smaller start-ups. One difference, of course, is the lure of equity positions in the form of stock options offered to employees in those burgeoning startups; many of those employees will trade off sleep and any semblance of a "normal" life today for the possibility of striking it rich when the startup's IPO happens.

The other difference is the extent to which traditional corporate and organizational values and norms create a work context that is less and less appealing today. It strikes me as a sad situation when the biggest single weapon most established firms have with which to change those old cultures is the adoption of full-time casual dress codes. The assumption seems to be that if employees are freed from the constrictions of neckties and high heels they will be eternally grateful, instantly empowered, and fully energized. This is nonsense.

The requirement to wear formal business clothing may be the most *tangible, visible* vestige of old-world thinking, but it is far from the only example of what distinguishes a *Fortune* 100 company from a dot-com startup. The inches-thick policies manuals, office size and decor that are directly proportional to job levels, and reserved parking spots for executives are only three ways in which employees are reminded every day of the weight of tradition and history. It is a weight that fewer and fewer are willing to endure.

How the Corporate Need for Speed Will Drive Mobile-Technology Use

There will be interesting ways in which some of the business trends noted above will merge with, or be influenced by, the technology trends. A fascinating and perhaps somewhat troubling perspective on this merger comes from Stamford, Connecticut–based Gartner Group Inc., one of the most highly respected advisory and consulting firms that tracks technology developments. Gartner Group has been following the growth of remote-access and mobile office technologies for years, and conducts an annual international conference on these themes.

Ken Dulaney, Gartner's vice president and research area director responsible for notebook computers, PDAs, cell phones, and related devices and technologies, predicted at the firm's 2000 conference on remote-access strategies that "by 2004, 60 percent of mobile workers will be compelled to carry technologies that offer instant response by voice and hourly response by e-mail." If he is correct, we will see an almost inexorable pressure on mobile workers simply because the availability of advanced technologies will feed

The Stomach Test: Your Readiness to Find the Off Switch

As we look ahead to your own future prospects for being able to draw some more clear boundaries between work and the rest of your life, ask yourself how deeply you believe the following five statements.

Choose one of these answers for each:
A. My head says "yes" but my gut says "no way."
B. My head says "yes" but my gut says "I'm not sure."
C. My head says "yes" and my gut agrees.

1. The first step in redrawing the boundaries is my own commitment to change; this isn't up to my manager or my employer to initiate. _____
2. Just because technology lets me work just about anytime and anyplace, I really shouldn't feel compelled to do so. _____
3. I'm being paid primarily for what I know and what I can do, not for working a certain number of hours or being endlessly responsive. _____
4. Most if not all the people I deal with will respect and support my intention to draw some boundaries around my work and my availability. _____
5. The number of e-mail messages I send or receive—and how many of them occur at night or on the weekend—really isn't a valid measure of my importance or worth. _____

You know how to score these questions; the more A and B answers you have, the more you still have some underlying doubts or skepticism about whether you can make these changes. Go back and look at the questions that earned those answers and ask yourself why you have the disconnect between what you believe to be true in your head but still can't accept as being actually true for you in the pit of your stomach. This, together with your answers to the "Six Predictors" below, will help you understand how easy it will be to establish and maintain the kind of work-life boundaries that you prefer.

everyone's expectations for faster response time. This strongly suggests that employees may be engaged in a tug-of-war between what the technology will enable and what they will prefer in terms of separation of work and the rest of their lives.

Six Predictors of *Your* Ability to "Turn It Off"

Having offered some observations and speculations about the future of technology and the pressures on (and resources of) employers and employees, I'll end this chapter with my list of the six factors that will predict how likely it is that employees like you will be able to craft and implement the kind of three-zones model we have been discussing. As you go through the list, write down after each item how well it describes you and your situation.

All else being equal, employees of an organization are *more* likely to successfully create and maintain their three-zones model if the following conditions apply:

- •Business Is Good. No surprise here; a healthy business environment allows employers to be more lenient and encourages them to be more responsive to what their employees want. This will be seen at a company- or industry-wide level, but probably not in an entire country. If the economy suffers for the country overall there will still be sectors that are thriving.

    This describes my situation (circle one):

    very well   somewhat   very little

- •Their Managers Are Young. At the risk of infuriating managers around my age (early 50s) or older, I think that those of us sneaking up on senior citizenship will have a harder time grappling with these issues of corporate response to the desire for work-life balance and integration. We didn't grow up with the technology that is so integral to the lives of those a generation or more younger than we are. For the most part, we had managed in our formative early years to separate work and the rest of our lives simply because we separated the work*place* from the rest of our lives. So, working for a younger manager might be a real plus in the ability to draw some boundaries.

    This describes my situation (circle one):

    very well   somewhat   very little

- •Their Skills Are Valued and Scarce. The traditional workings of a labor market that is alternatively a buyer's or a seller's market depending on the relative shortage of jobs or workers have not been replaced by the Internet. Show me someone who has hot skills and whose current or potential employer has a business-critical need for those skills, and I'll show you someone who stands a much better chance of getting whatever he or she wants from the employment relationship—with little or no regard for the type of industry involved.

This describes my situation (circle one):

very well   somewhat   very little

- **They Make and Keep Service-Level Commitments.** You are much more likely to be able to carve out some "mid-duty" and "off duty" periods each week if you can clearly state what your availability and response commitments are during your "on duty" and "mid-duty" periods—*and* if you honor those commitments. It is far worse to have others expect you to be accessible and available, only to find out that you aren't, than it is if they didn't expect to have contact with you at all. If your history with others (primarily your boss and your most important co-workers and clients) is such that they can accurately predict your availability and responsiveness at any given time, your odds of being able to create more "off duty" time go up significantly.

This describes my situation (circle one):

very well   somewhat   very little

- **They Have and Can Use Broadband Network Access.** You have seen my bias toward the importance of telecommunications in the future of technology in the workplace. Without denying the technological marvels that are today's notebook computers, cell phones, PDAs, and all the rest that we have and will soon have, they all become almost useless unless they are connected to the public Internet and the corporate intranets and extranets—and connected at speeds close to if not the same as what's provided by hard-wired access in the office. You won't have the option to decide how well and for how long you can work anytime and anywhere unless you *can* work anytime, anywhere.

This describes my situation (circle one):

very well   somewhat   very little

- They Have Good Negotiation and Presentation Skills. The amount of emphasis I put on the process (in Chapter 6) of discussing your three-zones model with your boss and others tells you how crucial it is to be able to hold that conversation comfortably and confidently. The definition of the three zones, and what they mean, will in my view primarily be a bottom-up, employee-driven process. The person doesn't need to go into that discussion with a six-megabyte presentation file and streaming video; this isn't a case where those bells and whistles make much of a difference. Instead, this situation requires good old-fashioned personal communications skills that blend the ability to make and present a business case with equal doses of assertion, empathy, and listening ability. Not a very high-tech, new-millennium prescription, I'm afraid, but we are still people with emotions and feelings talking to other people with emotions and feelings. If that kind of communication skill is missing, I believe the employee will be at a great disadvantage.

This describes my situation (circle one):

very well   somewhat   very little

What Does the Future (and *Your* Future) Look Like?

Although you were asked to rate those six factors from your own perspective, you can just as easily do it for your organization in general; this lets you assess how likely it is that people across the organization will be able to implement the three-zones model. If you choose to look at how you rated those six factors for your own situation, the prediction applies more specifically to you. In either case, use the following (non-scientific) scoring to produce a total for yourself or for your organization.

Add up the number of ratings for each answer choice, write the totals in the left column, and multiply by the scores listed:

____ Describes *very well* $\times 5 =$ ____

____ Describes *somewhat* $\times 2 =$ ____

____ Describes *very little* $\times 0 =$ ____

(must total *6*)   Grand Total = ____

If your Grand Total is 20 or higher, your chances of being successful with your own work-life time plan are very good. If it is between 15 and 19, your chances of being successful with your own work-life time plan are so-so. And if your Grand Total is below 15, you probably can expect to be working on a schedule and in places that will be determined primarily by someone else.

You can see that I have skewed the weights very much in favor of the presence of the six factors, and with no weight assigned if a factor was rated as not very relevant. My rationale is simple: I don't think that you, or anyone, will be successful with this approach unless the factors are strongly evident. This isn't an all-or-nothing process, but it seems to me that you must have enough strengths in your favor to be able to make this happen completely, or else it just won't work. I don't think there's such a thing as being a "little bit" in control of the boundaries between your work and your life.

More important than my scoring weighting is your assessment of what this means for you. Look at the items that you rated as only somewhat or minimally descriptive of your situation, and ask yourself what you can do to influence or control them. If you are doing this exercise for yourself, then the "influence or control" factors are those you can effect. If you are looking at this for your entire organization, you're dealing with broader issues that might not always be under your control. I don't claim that this analysis is fully predictive, but I do believe it points you in the right direction to see what the near-term future holds for you.

CHAPTER 9

WHAT TO DO IF YOU JUST CAN'T

"TURN IT OFF"

You've made it this far, so you're obviously serious about learning about how you use your time and about whether you can establish some boundaries between work and the rest of your life. If all went well, you developed a good action plan, put forth the right amount and type of effort to implement it, and got the results you wanted.

But—in Case You Didn't . . .

Despite your best efforts to this point, however, it's possible that you *didn't* achieve what you would have liked in terms of how to turn your time use and your life around. Maybe you just can't wean yourself off all that technology, and in fact, maybe your life now revolves completely around e-mail, cell phones, and the like.

If you still find yourself spending too much time being chased by too much technology, and with too little time to devote to your own needs, there are three possible explanations:

- Good Plan, Good Effort, Unsatisfactory Results. You carefully analyzed your current time use and identified your goals, thought through how you'd approach your boss and co-workers/clients, and had everything in place to achieve your goals—but you still find yourself spending too much time working on weekends and you can't seem to get unhooked from your electronic tether.

- Good Plan, Unsuccessful Effort, Unsatisfactory Results. You started off on the right foot—with good analysis and good goal setting—but for some reason fell short on implementation. Perhaps you weren't able to get the support and commitment you needed from your boss and others who influence your time use. Perhaps you didn't carve out enough time for your "mid-duty" and "off duty" zones. Or perhaps the business conditions in your organization changed dramatically and now *everyone* seems to be working almost nonstop.

- Inadequate Plan, Unsuccessful Effort, Unsatisfactory Results. This is the most difficult possibility to consider. It's conceivable that you just didn't spend enough time on your initial analysis or weren't as honest with yourself about how you use your time and what effect that time use has on you, your work, and your significant others. If so, it would have been almost impossible to come up with a meaningful action plan, and thus the results you got were less than what you would have wanted.

At this point, you have the option of retracing your steps back through Chapters 2 through 5, and in particular taking a second look at how you developed your own three-zones model in Chapter 5. This might help you get some fresh insights into what's needed to bring the changes you want. On the other hand, it's possible that there's something about your situation that, for now, makes it very difficult if not impossible for you to create the kind of breathing room you want.

Why *Can't* You "Turn It Off"?

There is an endless list of possible answers to that question. Here are some of the most likely explanations for why you might not have been able to create some change in how you divide up your week between work and the rest of your life:

- Perhaps your *employer* is facing some very serious and urgent pressures to fight off a competitive challenge, launch a new product, or deal with a customer-service problem. You're right in the middle of the battle to address this and there's no way (short of resigning) to avoid these pressures.
- Perhaps your *manager* just doesn't care about how these time-use issues affect you, or isn't willing to be responsive to your requests for help and support.
- Perhaps your *co-workers or clients* are relentless in their pursuit of you, your evenings and weekends, and your

expertise. They might be overly dependent on you or have expectations for access and availability that are unrealistic, but which you can't change.

• Finally, perhaps *you* are contributing to or even causing your own problems. Is it your personality, your dedication, your uncertainties about your job, your unwillingness to delegate to others—who knows? I can't peer into your psyche to find the answers to those questions; I'm not qualified to do that, and it's not the purpose of this chapter or this book.

No matter what you decide about the possible *cause*, the *result* is the same: you end up spending more time than you would like answering voice mail and e-mail messages, responding to pages and phone calls, and otherwise engaged in work instead of something else you'd rather do. Maybe this is just a temporary situation; for example, if you're facing the immediacy of the kind of business pressure noted above, it's possible that you might regain some more control over your time use when that crisis is over a few weeks or months from now.

Maybe the boss who is now standing between you and the kind of three-zones model you'd like will move on, move up, or move out. I've met several people over the years who said they solved their bad-boss problem by surreptitiously passing the boss's name on to a headhunter who then recruited the boss away to a new job. That tactic may not work every time, but I can see how someone who likes his or her job and employer more than the boss might be tempted to do this.

Whatever the cause and whatever the effect it has on you,

What Does Not Working Mean to You?

From an early age we're surrounded by messages about the importance of work and the obligation we have to do that work. These become subconscious behavior cues that can drive us to work more than we'd like and to feel guilty when we aren't working.

It may help you to become more aware of some of those messages and how they might be affecting your ability to turn it off. Here are two lists of synonyms—one for "work" and one for "play." Read through each list and circle the words that jump out, words that for you are the deeper connotations of "work" and "play":

Work		Play	
Task	Assignment	Amusement	Diversion
Chore	Duty	Distraction	Enjoyment
Effort	Mission	Entertainment	Fun
Responsibility	Achievement	Game	Pleasure
Fulfillment	Satisfaction	Excitement	Happiness
Success	Obligation	Hobby	Elation
Accountability	Burden		

All "work" isn't drudgery and punishment, and all "play" isn't happiness and excitement—and the choices we make to spend time at play rather than at work shouldn't necessarily lead to guilt, also known as regret, remorse, fault, shame, and burden. . . .

the result is the same: you simply are not able to create better or different boundaries between your work and your life no matter what you try.

Don't Give Up Hope—Cope!

You have three options at this point if you simply aren't able to cut the cord and create enough "mid-duty" and "off duty" time to satisfy you:

1. Put It on Hold. It's possible that you just need to declare a "time out" to let all these issues settle before making any other decisions. You might want to put this entire topic out of your mind and revisit it later. If so, commit to yourself that you'll tackle the issue again at a specific time—say, six weeks from today—rather than just saying, "I'll get to it sometime." If this sounds like a reasonable approach, take out your calendar or PDA right *now* and make a note of your follow-up date. Call this an "appointment with me"—it could be one of the most important appointments you'll have all year.

2. Seek Professional or Other Help. If you want to make some changes and have done what you feel is your best but still don't have the results you seek, perhaps you need someone or some other resources to help you through this process. There's no need to feel uncomfortable about asking for help; making a change in long-standing habits and patterns is never easy.

Your resources range from good friends, mentors, family members, and co-workers to counselors you can find through your employer's Employee Assistance Program (if available), other professional counselors, psychologists, or psychiatrists, or career-management advisers.

There are also online support and information resources available,* especially for so-called workaholics. That term connotes a kind of addiction to work that is not necessarily at the root of someone's attachment to technology as we've been discussing. However, resources such as these might be helpful for general guidance:

- Yahoo! has a message board and chat room for recovering workaholics <clubs.yahoo.com/clubs/recoveringwork aholics>.
- eGroups™ <www.egroups.com/group/worka> has a similar message board.
- There's an unofficial Web site for Workaholics Anonymous <people.ne.mediaone.net/wa2/index.html>, which includes this description of how Workaholics Anonymous got started:

WA was started in April 1983 by a New York corporate financial planner and a school teacher, who had been "hopeless" work addicts. They founded WA in an effort to help others who suffered from the disease of workaholism and to stop working compulsively themselves. They were joined in their first

---

*Online resources such as these change frequently; use a search engine to check what's available and accessible to you.

meeting by the spouse of the planner, who started Work-Anon, a program of recovery for those in a relationship with a workaholic.

Though I have included various kinds of counseling or therapeutic professionals in this list of possible resources, this does not imply that you're sick, defective, weak, or otherwise unable to cope with this issue yourself. The subject of work-life boundary setting can be more complex than it seems, and it sometimes helps to bring in the views and suggestions of someone who is trained to help people find solutions to problems like these. A professional counselor isn't going to "fix" you—because you aren't broken. All that person will do is help you understand your current situation a little better and then help you craft and implement your own plan to change what you want to change.

3. Admit Defeat and Make the Best of It. If, for whatever reason, you just can't get away from work and all of its electronic tentacles, so be it. You tried, you might give it another attempt later on, but at this point you have to make the best of things.

Learning How to *Not* Work

Before you give up on your attempts to rein in your work hours and demands, maybe you can try one last tactic for breaking away from the near-endless work you face.

We all spend years learning how to do our jobs, how to meet deadlines, and, in general, how to *produce*. The more stringent our job demands, the more likely it is that the ability to relax, play, and do nothing that we all had as children or teenagers gets hidden away or disappears entirely.

If you're serious about trying to keep your job within the boundaries you'd like to set, maybe it's time to relearn how to do *nothing*—or at least, how to relax while doing something other than work. This sounds simple and logical, but it's not always easy to do. One way to make it easier is to attack it like a business problem; ironic as that may seem, it might be the best way for hard-charging businesspeople to learn how to get unplugged. Consider these alternatives:

1. Schedule Your Relaxation Time. We're all so schedule-obsessed and driven by our calendars; maybe the way to fit in some relaxation is to treat it like any other calendar commitment. It sounds odd, perhaps, but try making your own weekly time budget for relaxation. For example, try planning to spend 30 minutes each evening reading for pleasure or enjoying your favorite hobby; schedule an hour on a weekend to work on your backswing at a golf driving range, and so on. Putting these "play" activities on the calendar elevates them in importance and also may help you fill what otherwise would be free time with work time.

2. Manage Your "Me" Projects. Maybe you've always wanted to learn to play the piano, brush up on a foreign language, or follow any other pursuit that you think you'll enjoy but don't have the time for. Consider the advice of Alan Lakein, the time-management expert cited in Chapter 4: he advocates the "Swiss cheese" method for dividing those big, overwhelming tasks into smaller, more manageable ones.

Lakein contends that one reason most of us avoid the big and important tasks we face is that we can't conceive of ever finding enough time to tackle them. As a result, we spend lots of 10- or 20-minute blocks of time working on tasks that are far less important; this gives us the satisfaction of crossing items off our to-do list, but it doesn't help us make any progress on the more important things we need to accomplish.

He suggests that we carve up those big, overwhelming tasks or projects into smaller pieces that can be extracted from the whole—creating a kind of "Swiss cheese" effect in which that big block is now much less formidable. When you have ten minutes free, use it to do a small part of that big task instead of opting for something less important. At the end of the ten minutes, you're that much closer to completing the top-priority project.

Instead of applying this method to your work, however, use it for your piano-playing skills, or your Italian language refresher, or anything else that's enjoyable but too big to find one large block of time to accomplish. For example, you won't be able to learn a piano concerto in ten minutes, but you can certainly work on some basic fingerings and scales. Then the next time you have 10 or 20 minutes available in the evening or on the weekend, you can build on what you learned and move forward.

3. Find Pleasure on Your PC. If you're really addicted to your computer and just can't stand being separated from it, let that urge work to your advantage by using the PC and the power of the Internet to engage you in some non-work activities. (I'm not suggesting you do this at work, however, and even if you wanted to do that, employers are becoming increasingly diligent about monitoring employees' use of PCs for non-work purposes and reprimanding or disciplining them

accordingly. I'm not sure I agree with that strategy, but the fact is that it exists so don't use your work time in the workplace this way.)

Let's say that you're sitting at home at night or on the weekend, or you're on an airplane, and feel the inexorable desire to power up the PC and tackle some work that needs to be done. Instead, consider these or similar activities that will let you get your hands on the keyboard without doing any actual work:

- Use CD-ROM instructional software to work on that foreign language you want to learn or brush up on, plot out the design for your summer cottage or new home, perfect your bridge-playing strategies, or any one of thousands of other applications.
- Visit Web sites dealing with family genealogy, foreign countries you'd like to visit, your college alumni association, the latest political analysis, or any one of literally millions of other Web sites.
- Get back in touch with distant relatives, former neighbors, long-lost college buddies, or anyone else who'd be pleasantly surprised to get a long letter from you.
- Allow me to share with you some photographs I've taken on various hiking trips throughout the Southwest, and accompanying nature texts and personal notes. As described on the "Natural Escape" section of my Web site <www.gilgordon.com/escape/current/index.htm>, I find these photographs doubly relaxing: once when I took them, and again—and again—when I view them on the site.

These are only four of dozens of ways to use your computer for something other than work. I realize it may seem a little counterintuitive to suggest that you put your hands on the keyboard of the machine you may desperately be trying to avoid as part of your boundary-setting strategy. But if that's what works for you as a kind of transitional activity, it's much better than doing nothing at all.

Working on the Road—and on the Plane, the Ship, and Elsewhere

If you're resigned to the fact that you just can't seem to find that off switch, especially when you're away from the office, you can take some comfort in knowing that your prospects for working on the go are better than ever.

In fact, if you're traveling for business *or* pleasure, you're likely to have everything you need to keep up with the work you just can't seem to escape. There have been telephones on airplanes for almost a decade. Many airports, and most major hotels and resorts, offer business centers on site with photo-copying, computers, and printers for rent, and more. Guest rooms in hotels that cater to business travelers provide extra phone jacks, desks and chairs suited for long periods of desk work, and increasingly, high-speed Internet access. By now, this is old hat—it's the exception today to find a hotel that doesn't offer these amenities.

But what about the times when you're away from the home, office, or typical business venues and you absolutely need to get some work done—even if you're in a decidedly non-work setting? For starters, there is a worldwide network of "Internet cafés" or "telecenters" where business travelers can drop in and check e-mail or work on a rented computer; you can find a list of these on my Web site <www.gilgordon. com/telecommuting/mobileaccess.htm>. You'd be surprised how easy it is to find high-speed Internet access in some of the most remote towns in countries all over the world.

For better or worse, the list of work-friendly locations seems to be growing beyond our wildest expectations. Instead of fretting over how you *won't* be able to get away from work so you can enjoy the rest of life, here are some ways and places you can enjoy the rest of life without getting away from work. These suggestions aren't meant to be all-inclusive, and I am not endorsing or recommending any of these products, services, or companies. This is just a sample of some of the ways the marketplace is responding to the desire to combine work and personal time.

1. Ski and Surf: Whistler Mountain, a popular ski area in British Columbia, Canada, has a "business communication center" at the top of the mountain. Monitors show global stock updates, computers are available for checking e-mail or going onto the Internet, a fax machine stands ready to send or receive, and there's even a small conference room available for meetings that just can't wait.

2. Fly and Fax. Malaysia Airlines now offers an on-board business center on some of its aircraft. As noted on the airline's Web site, "Our B-777 SuperRanger Series features a computerized Business Center for use of our First Class, Business Class and MAS Esteemed traveler members. It's like

an office in the sky, complete with multimedia-ready computer, business and travel guides, printer and fax machines, and satellite telephones."

3. Sail and Surf. Norwegian Cruise Lines' *Norwegian Sky* ship set sail in August 1999 and became the first cruise ship with an on-board Internet café. This "office on the waves" was installed in the entire fleet as of February 2000. The Internet Café aboard all ships is available for use on a 24-hour-a-day basis; guests can send and receive e-mail messages, check the stock market, get news updates, play computer games, and more. Competition being what it is, Royal Caribbean International also offers a similar service on its ships, boasting of leading the "@Sea Revolution with the largest digital cruise fleet."

4. Swim and Scribble. Cruising might not be on your social calendar, but if you're floating in the pool, swimming laps, or out on your boat and have an urge to make some notes about that big project, you can simply reach for the Circa H_2O Notebook, offered by Levenger. "Our new Circa H_2O Notebook allows you to take notes in all kinds of conditions: doing professional field work in inclement weather, or while boating, skiing, bird-watching, or gardening. The synthetic cover protects your musings, and the 50 sheets of Kimdura plastic-coated paper will preserve your thoughts," notes the company.

5. Drive and Do a Deal. Rather than even bother looking around for a place to do some office work while you're on the go, why not just take your office with you? A number of manufacturers can outfit a van or even a full-size bus as a mobile office. For example, LandJet Inc. will put these gadgets into a van to give you a true office on wheels:

Power ports for cellular telephones;

Power ports for laptop computers;

A combination fax machine, copier, printer, and modem;

A satellite communications dish;

A global positioning, navigating, and tracking system;

A 13-inch color television;

A videocassette recorder;

A six-disc compact disc player;

An AM/FM stereo radio/cassette player;

A Surround-Sound speaker system;

A refrigerator;

A microwave oven.

As noted on the company's Web site, there's no such thing as wasted travel time any longer. "In a LandJet, 'on the road' no longer means 'out of touch.' With the world's most advanced mobile business electronics at your fingertips, once wasted down-time now becomes an opportunity to catch up, or win clients, sell product or convince customers. Alternatively, you can read and work on documents, or just comfortably recline, reduce the stress of your day, and think creative thoughts."

6. Build Muscles *and* Business. Last but not least, you can even do your work while you're working out. Netpulse Communications Inc. provides the "Internet-Powered Workout." The company "transforms health club exercise bikes, steppers, and ellipticals with a sleek, flat touch-screen control panel and a high-speed Internet connection to deliver a whole new kind of workout—the Internet Powered Workout." While you're stepping or pedaling away the pounds and getting your heart rate going, you can have the following at your sweaty fingertips:

Fast Web access to news updates, entertainment sites,
   sports scores, stock quotes, shopping, and more;

Personal TV;

Built-in audio CD player;

Workout tracking to review progress over time;

State-of-the-Art Design and Cutting-Edge Technology;

High-speed Internet connectivity;

Sleek, flat panel touch-screen controls with a 17-inch
   monitor.

Does this mean your heart rate would vary with the interest
rates? Would you step faster if you get angry reading
e-mail from your boss? We might have an entirely new set
of work-related strains and stresses to deal with just because we're exercising our brains and our bodies at the
same time.

Now—on to *Your* Future

You might have come to the conclusion that all this cruising,
skiing, and sweating isn't the most desirable way to do your
office work. Or perhaps you came away from that last section
completely enthused about how you *can* have it all, do it
all, and fully integrate work and the rest of your life without
missing a beat. No matter where you stand on the work-life
separation scale, you've come almost to the end of this explo-
ration of why and how you might be able to "turn it off" and
have the option to create some different boundaries between
work and personal time.

Chapter 1 began with this paragraph:

> None of us wakes up one day and decides, "I think
> I'll give up my free time on weekends, answer my
> pages during dinner with my spouse, and carry my
> laptop on vacation." Those intrusions of work into
> our personal time result from a process of slow
> erosion, not sudden upheaval. As employees, we
> ourselves have unwittingly contributed to that
> process and ended up stretching our workdays
> and workweeks.

The implication of that paragraph is that many of us—perhaps inadvertently—end up getting our priorities wrong. No matter how we rationalize and justify all those work hours, the result is the same: more hours spent working means fewer hours available for living outside of work. I'll close with the following parable that makes this point crystal-clear:

> One day an expert in time management was speaking
> to a group of business students and, to drive home a
> point, used an illustration those students will never
> forget. As he stood in front of the group of high-
> powered overachievers he said, "Okay, time for a
> quiz." Then he pulled out a one-gallon, widemouthed
> jar and set it on the table in front of him. He pro-
> duced about a dozen fist-sized rocks and carefully
> placed them, one at a time, into the jar. When the jar
> was filled to the top and no more rocks would fit
> inside, he asked, "Is this jar full?"

Everyone in the class said, "Yes."

Then he said, "Really?" He reached under the table and pulled out a bucket of gravel. Then he dumped some gravel in and shook the jar causing pieces of gravel to work themselves down into the space between the big rocks. He asked the group once more, "Is the jar full?"

By this time the class was on to him. "Probably not," one of them answered.

"Good!" he replied. He reached under the table and brought out a bucket of sand. He started dumping the sand in the jar and it went into all of the spaces left between the rocks and the gravel. Once more he asked the question: "Is this jar full?"

"No!" the class shouted.

Once again he said, "Good." He grabbed a pitcher of water and began to pour it in until the jar was filled to the brim. Then he looked at the class and asked, "What is the point of this illustration?"

One eager beaver raised his hand and said, "The point is, no matter how full your schedule is, if you try really hard you can always fit some more things in it!"

"No," the speaker replied, "that's not the point. What this illustration teaches us is: If you don't put the big rocks in first, you'll never get them in at all."

What are the "big rocks" in your life? Your children? Your loved ones? Your education? Your dreams? A worthy cause? Teaching or mentoring others? Doing things that you love? Time for yourself? Your health? Your significant other?

Remember to put these *big rocks* in first. If you sweat the little stuff (the gravel, the sand, the water), then you'll fill your life with and worry about the little things that don't really matter, and you'll never have the real quality time you need to spend on the big, important stuff—the big rocks.

So, tonight, or in the morning, when you are reflecting on this short story, ask yourself this question: What are the "big rocks" in my life? Then put those in your jar first.

My "big rocks" are my health, my family, my sense of satisfaction with and the enjoyment I get from my work, and my time spent out in the wilderness. I've tried to put them in my jar first, and I have succeeded more often than not. Writing this book has reminded me of those priorities and of the need to keep making those conscious decisions about time use based on them. I hope it accomplishes the same for you.

Looking for More Information?

Thank you for your purchase of this book; I hope you found it useful and thought-provoking.

   If you're interested in finding out more about *Turn It Off* topics and developments, please register at <www.turnitoff.